Scorpio x 10

A Story of Healing

Victoria Pendragon

Copyright © 2023
All Rights Reserved

This book is dedicated to every person who has ever experienced childhood sexual abuse. Speak openly where that is appropriate because abusers count on their victims to remain silent. It is exactly what allows them to continue their heinous actions. They will try to make you feel as though you deserve to be ashamed of what happened to you just to keep you quiet. You have nothing to be afraid of. Speak up. Speak out.

Acknowledgement

I owe a debt of thanks to Marina at Darkstar Astrology for explaining to me, as gently as possible, that with Chiron sitting on my Scorpio ascendent, three planets, three asteroids, the sun and the moon all cuddled up in Scorpio in the first house of my chart, Pluto conjunct Saturn conjunct at midheaven, and my north node snuggling into Uranus in the 8th house that there was little chance I'd have had any other kind of life than the one I've led. It was information I'd waited my whole life to hear, the answer to my ever-present questions: Why? Why me? Why this?

"*Scorpio thrives on real truth—and the real truth is in short supply in the social world.*" The Book of Water, Steven Forrest

This is a true story.

Table of Contents

Mouse 1

Nana & Pop-Pop 5

Manoa 10

Merion 15

Vaginas & Other Things... 20

The Accident 40

Back To School.. 51

A New Year's Day To Remember 57

A Trip To The Mountains 60

Dancing & Art Classes 62

Play Farm Day Camp 69

One Last Time... 73

Christmas 81

A Trip To Cuba 85

Ocean City 97

Moving, Changing Schools 108

More Damn Dance Classes 122

Expanding Horizons.. 133

Exploring Relationship..139

Nether Providence...145

New School, New Friends 158

Prom..163

The Long-Distance Relationship...172

College 178

Looking For Help.. 193

Rape 207

Help?.. 211

Picking Up Where She Left Off... 220

Penland 223

Annie.. 232

Back To School... & Beyond 235

The Wedding 249

Settling In 252

New Things 261

Expanding.. 265

Coping.. 278

Health Issues... 294

Laying Foundations 296

Reality Kicks In 308

Moving... 316

Another Path To Walk 324

Treatment.. 328

Power Animals & An Invitation 342

Strong Now.. 354

Free At Last?.. 364

Expanding.. 373

Two Steps Forward And Oops... 378

Moving... 380

A Brief And Unpleasant Winterlude 385

More Moving 388
Epilogue: Healing 420

Mouse

"At a certain period of the worm's life, its outer skin hardens, and within what has become a chrysalis, a process of utter disintegration occurs until the chrysalis is only a hard skin filled with a jellied substance. But out of this apparently inchoate jelly, the butterfly will soon form the glory of wings." The Astrology of Personality, Dane Rudhyar, 1936.

This *is* a true story. The incidents and history are related exactly as they were, although names have been changed in an attempt to calm down those who may be embarrassed by the story, annoyed by it, or who would prefer to remain in denial. Perhaps, to quote Macbeth, "It is a tale told by an idiot, full of sound and fury and signifying nothing." Whatever it may be, it is, at any rate, the story of Mouse, who was once a real girl who got lost in the process of becoming but finally found her way home... to herself.

Prelude

The doctors Polly White and Guillermo Garcia-Martinez were married in the chapel of the Hospital of the University of Pennsylvania in April of 1945. They remained married until their divorce in 1982.

1946

Mouse was born in 1946 under the influence of the then commonly used drug, Twilight Sleep, a potent mixture of morphine and scopolamine that not only eliminated the mother's pain but also relieved her of any memory of the experience and, as you would suspect, drugged the infant as well. The standard whack on the baby's back was not enough to get the newly born tiny girl baby breathing and she had to be resuscitated.

In light of the life that she, the baby, Mouse, was about to experience, there is some chance that she had simply been looking for an easy out.

For the first few months of her life, Mouse spent her days in the arms of a caring older woman named Mrs. Waar and her nights with her parents in a tiny apartment they rented over a jewelry store on Sansom

Street in Philadelphia, an area that is still known as Jewelers Row. Her tiny bassinet was kept in the shower and when she woke, she would wiggle about, as babies do, reaching out and grabbing at the walls of her container. Her sharp little nails would scratch against the protective plastic that lined the sides. It took a few days before her parents realized that the sound that they were hearing was their infant daughter and not, as they had suspected, a mouse. Thus, it was that she acquired her name.

1947

Before she was even six months old, Mouse acquired tuberculosis from her mother, Polly, who had, apparently, contracted it in the hospital morgue where she, as a newly minted pathologist, had been plying her trade. There was, at the time, no cure for tuberculosis save that of resting a lot and hoping—or praying—for the best. Polly—who'd been given the nickname Rabbit by her med school classmates—was sent to endure recuperation at the luxurious home of her in-laws in Havana, Cuba, where she could take in the healing properties of the sun every day and be waited on hand and foot.

Because there was no cure for tuberculosis and because infants unlucky enough to contract it generally died from it, Mouse was put on loan to the very same hospital which had gifted her with the disease. She would serve as a guinea pig for the drugs that were being developed in the search for a potential cure. Her father, now "Daddy," visited her regularly and won the hearts of all the young nurses as he carried his little daughter around the nursery, patting her back and cooing to her. Daddy was of a type then known as "The Latin Lover," and he made every effort to live up to his title.

Meanwhile, in Havana, Mommy/Rabbit realized that she was, once again, with child. By the time she was healthy enough to return to the states, Mouse, who'd been fortunate enough to receive the one drug that had worked, had become free of the disease and had been sent off to live with her maternal grandparents "for the time being."

Nana & Pop-Pop

Long ago, Marie and Edgar, aka Nana and Pop-Pop—Polly's mother and father—had produced three children: two boys and a girl. Pop-pop had come from a very, very troublesome background. His parents had died before he was even school-age and he had been raised by one of his aunts. Mouse could only gather from the stories she would later hear, that she had not been a very nice person and that she also took a lot of medications.

Pop-pop was smart, though, and had studied hard in school. He was especially interested in electrical things and ended up working with a man named Thomas Edison. Eventually, he became involved with moviemaking and made a great deal of money. He had one home in Beverly Hills, another in the mountains in Pennsylvania, and another on the beach in Ocean City, New Jersey. He had many wealthy friends and became used to a standard of living that was much, much better than the situation he had endured as a child or, for that matter, much, much better than most people in the country.

But the financial crash of 1929 had ruined him. He'd lost the home in Beverly Hills and was forced to downsize the mountain home to an apartment in Pottsville, Pennsylvania. He established his three-story home at the shore as his main residence, renting out the lower two floors to pay the mortgage. That was enough to get by, but he felt as if he needed more, so when he became involved in a car accident one day that had been serious enough to have landed him in the hospital briefly, he left the hospital on crutches and never walked without them again… at least, not where anyone could see him. In private, in his workroom, which was windowless, he hung the canes up on a hook on the wall and went about his business like the fully functional person that he actually was. He collected insurance payments for the rest of his life on the grounds that the accident had crippled him. He never drove again; his wife would always chauffer him in their Cadillac. His wife had been born into a wealthy family, and nothing less than the best car that they could buy would suit either of them.

When his children came of school age, he informed each of them that they were to become doctors and that if they did not attend medical school, he would disown them. His reasoning, he explained, was that he did not want to see his children 'suffer' as he had and that, as physicians, they would never be put into a position where their income would be in danger.

Aside from that, he seemed to have treated his children with as much respect as he had ever treated anyone, which is to say that he felt free to use them as pawns. His daughter, Mouse's mother, who was called Polly by everyone, had been a brilliant child, easily outstripping her classmates in school. Her father saw this as a plus when it came to her ability to generate income more quickly and, whenever he could, insisted that her teachers allow her to skip a grade… or, perhaps more correctly, that they allow him to have his wish that she skip grades regularly. That had never been Polly's wish and she was miserable. Her diary revealed a very sad child who had few friends because she kept having to leave them behind every time she was forced forward and she'd ended up years younger than her classmates. She spent more time studying than doing anything else. Only in the summertime did she get a bit of a break. Since she'd known practically no one in her own class at school as she was "too young" for them, she was limited to "summertime friends." These were the kids whose parents took them to the shore for a few weeks or, as in the case of her "best friend," Grace Kelly, people whose families would spend the entire summer there. Grace's family lived in a marvelous, Spanish-style home that was also just off the beach and just down the road from Polly. So, at least for the summer months, Polly had a friend.

When the Second World War broke out and Polly's brothers "joined up," their paychecks were sent home—for safekeeping—to their parents. Polly's parents, though, spent the money. The boys never saw a dime. Pop-Pop used the money to fund fabulous trips for himself and his wife, cruises, mostly, and expensive jewelry.

These were the people with whom Polly and Memo had chosen to leave their infant child. It should have been no surprise that when they went to Ocean City,

New Jersey, to reclaim their by-then almost-year-old baby girl, she had none of the usual baby skills that infants develop. Most infants, by then, will make attempts to push themselves up if they are lying on their tummies; many will show signs of preliminary crawling motions. The baby they met, wrapped tightly from the neck down in a small, lightweight blanket, had never been allowed to develop those rudimentary skills.

"She wiggled too much," said Polly's mother, and that was annoying to them, so she had been, for months, kept tightly swaddled.

Manoa

Polly and Memo had taken advantage of the time they had together after Polly's return to the states to go house hunting. They'd found a three-story house in a residential suburb of Philadelphia with a yard and a garage and, best of all, a cellar that had been converted into a kind of entertainment den. Polly and Memo were partiers and loved to entertain. In their own cellar, Memo could drink as much as he liked without having to worry about driving home.

They settled in, bought a second car, and became commuters, each heading off to their appointed hospitals in the city every morning. Polly was on the verge of giving birth again and not long after they moved in, her second child, another daughter, was born. Annie was fourteen months younger than Mouse, whose growth had been less than vigorous, and Annie caught up to her sister, size-wise, in no time. Polly dressed them as twins, enjoying the attention she garnered.

As the girls grew, playground equipment was added to the yard, a small swing set and a slide. Help was hired. Memo handled the interviews. Many were called, but the position was finally awarded to a stunningly beautiful black woman named Marjorie. Mommy made out a very explicit set of directions, complete with a time schedule for Marjorie to follow with regard to "the girls" activities and meals throughout the day.

One day, however, the established schedule had to be abandoned.

Down the street from their house, there lived a troublesome boy of about ten or eleven years old. He'd pass their yard every day on his way to and from school and would sometimes yell nasty things at the girls whose skin tone was more like their Cuban father's than like their Germanic mother's. One day, though, he took things a little farther.

Annie had been inside, napping. Mouse was doing rounds on the sliding board, running, and climbing, and sliding as fast as she could just to see how fast she could go. The boy came by, as he always did, and shouted slurs at her. Used to his behavior, Mouse ignored him, and he continued on his way.

Not long after, though, he returned, and this time, perhaps having seen that she was alone, he was carrying a knife. It was a sharp knife, the kind that a person might use to carve a roast. He opened the gate and walked right in as if he had every right to.

Mouse, who'd been just at the base of the ladder, turned and ran to what looked like her best option for escape. The kitchen door was way too far away and up a few stairs, but the garage door was only a couple of yards away. She was closer to the garage door than he was to her; she fled, got in and locked the door behind her. Then she ran as far away from the door as she could, searching for any of the many tools that she knew her father kept in the garage that she might be able to use as a weapon, but all the tools were locked in a big metal case. The sounds of the boy rattling the door were unnerving her.

She spotted a tin can sitting on the workbench. It had been opened with an old-fashioned can-opener, the sort that was like a very sharp hook with a handle that you had to rock back and forth to cut the metal. The lid of the can had been pushed back inside it as was often done to prevent someone from getting cut by the jagged edges... but she thought, *if I could get that lid back out... I could cut him.* Thinking no further than that, she jammed her right thumb, as hard as she could, to push past the lid so that she could hook it—so she thought—in the crook of her thumb and pull it out, forgetting, in her panic, that it was bound to cut her just as badly as she was hoping that it would cut him... and it did. Blood gushed out and her thumb was going nowhere. The ragged metal had locked into her, bone deep.

Knowing that things couldn't get any worse, she headed for the door and the mean boy that stood outside of it. He'd been waiting, but when he saw the blood, he turned away and ran as quickly as he could out of the yard.

Mouse then, with her good hand, unlocked the door and headed, as fast as she could go, shouting for Marjorie, towards the kitchen door. Marjorie had heard her screaming and the moment she saw what had happened, she ran for the phone, leaving Mouse to let herself in.

By the time the police arrived, Marjorie had wrapped Mouse's hand—tin can and offending lid still intact—in a towel, hoping to quell the flow of blood and had, as well, bundled up a half-asleep Annie. The policeman got them all into the back seat, not bothering to ask what had happened. The amount of blood everywhere and the mental state of both Marjorie and Mouse were apparently all he needed to know. He flipped on the siren and took off like life was dependent on it.

Mouse had passed out by the time they reached the emergency ward and the staff moved in a full-speed symphony of motion. The only thing Mouse would remember afterward was that someone had told her that she was going to see Mickey Mouse as a large black mask descended towards her face. The next thing she knew, she was home in bed, and it was the following day.

The mean boy never came back and shortly thereafter, they moved house.

Merion

The Rabbit—aka Mommy, aka Polly—was pregnant again and the house in Manoa had two strikes against it: the dangerous boy down the street and its distance from Center City Philadelphia, where both she and Memo worked. It was time, they reasoned, to move a little closer to work... and perhaps upgrade a little.

The house they decided upon was decidedly more up-scale than the house they were leaving, which had been nice enough but nothing really special. The house they'd found was, indeed, something special in a number of ways. For one thing, it was beautiful and had been built of stone. For another, it was located on what was termed "a private road," a far cry from the house in Manoa where a trolly ran down the middle of the street on a regular basis. No big trucks or busses were allowed on this road, and no through-traffic either.

The street was rather short by most standards—only about three city blocks long—and it made two sharp 90-degree turns—one, left and one, right—at about a block apart, turns that were to become a favorite spot for Memo to race up to at well way over the speed limit so that he could put his Porsche into a spin. The new house had what they called a sister house that was identical to it in every way and situated one block in from a main road, just as their new house was situated one block in from another main road called City Line where busses and trucks and many cars regularly traveled. There was even a small college across the big street from their private lane.

The sister houses had once served as offices for the private arboretum and art museum that spanned two of the blocks of the private lane and was well protected all around by a wrought iron fence, the spires of which were topped with pointed finials that promised pain to anyone who would attempt to scale the fence. A huge entrance gate was opened only for specific guests and deliveries, and just to make sure that no one attempted unauthorized entry, three seemingly vicious Dobermans roamed the property, paying special attention to the gate. Entry to the museum aspect of the property was by appointment only and, for some reason, the hours of operation had been reduced and it had been determined that staff could be cut so that only one of the two sister houses would be needed for the reduced staff. The other had been offered for sale and Memo had made the necessary arrangements to purchase it.

Memo had come from one of the wealthiest families in Cuba; he was more than used to the kind of luxury that was on offer. He'd haggled as much as he felt was appropriate, but he wanted that house, and he got it.

The property surrounding the house had been as thoughtfully landscaped as every part of the arboretum. The brick front walk perfectly punctuated a lawn which, on its left, edged a patch of ground ivy that led from the street to the raised outdoor porch that lay outside the dining room. Highlighting the demarcation line between the lawn and driveway stood a massive Copper Beech tree that was easily hundreds of years old. It was a beauty, and it became Mouse's favorite tree.

The side yard—the part of the property that had once connected it to the Foundation's property—was dotted with Honey Locust trees whose long, brown seed pods made perfect noisemakers when dried. The wrought iron fence, which continued from the road along the side of the property, made a striking backdrop for brilliant azalea bushes that blossomed with bright fuchsia flowers every spring. Back in the far corner of that side yard was Mouses' go-to hide-out, an unkempt gathering of forsythia bushes whose long, arched cascades of flowers provided privacy in the spring that she couldn't otherwise get.

This was where the faeries lived. Mouse couldn't see them, but she could feel their presence. She knew they were there, and she would sit amidst the bowers of yellow flowers in the spring, basking in the feel of them, in the knowledge of knowing that they were there. Angels, which her mother had told her about in church, she just couldn't buy into; they were too much people-sized to have wings and fly about... but tiny faeries she had no issues with; that seemed quite possible to her and, once she began hanging out in the bushes, it seemed quite real as well.

She knew about faeries because her mother was in the process of teaching her to read so that she would be prepared for school, and had made use of a particularly beautifully illustrated book on faeries and the flowers that they were associated with, and their house was surrounded by all kinds of flowering bushes. To Mouse, that meant faeries.

Vaginas & Other Things

Mouse was learning other things as well.

For instance, she had learned, at the doctor's office, that the place that Daddy and the doctor—at just that moment—had been putting his finger was called "a vagina." She got to learn that because sometimes she would get infections there and when that happened, she had to spend what seemed like forever to her sitting in purple water in a kind-of-a-bowl-thing called a sitz-bath that fit into the toilet in Daddy and Mommy's bathroom. They never even gave her a book to read, but she was afraid to ask for one because... well, just because she was small and they were in charge and if she was allowed to have a book, they would have offered it.

She learned, too, from her father what a penis was and how to make it happy with her tongue and her mouth. She liked that... a lot. It was as if she had this pet that she could make grow. And then it did things! It was a fountain! She especially enjoyed watching the television show where they had a penis, whose name was Willy, that wore a hat—and glasses—and had a friend that was a mouse. It was just like her and Daddy!

Mornings were nice in Mommy and Daddy's room, where Mouse often went after Mommy had left for work. Daddy would turn on the morning television shows for her, and Mouse would alternate watching them with watching her father get ready for his day. He'd always walk around naked, and Mouse was always completely captivated by the sight of his penis and testicles.

Mouse loved reading. It was her very favorite thing. She hadn't liked learning to read mostly because she didn't like to be told what to do or when, but she learned fast and once she did, she headed straight for the Books of Knowledge that were kept in the bedroom that she shared with Annie. She quickly moved up to the Encyclopedia Britannica that was kept in the formal living room on the bottom shelves of the built-in bookcase that rose clear to the ceiling. The dictionary was close at hand for all the words she didn't recognize, and she was in heaven. It was in the Encyclopedia

Britannica that she discovered things that fascinated her, some of which would stay with her until she was old. Yoga was one of those things.

There had been a photograph in the Encyclopedia of a very, very old and very, very skinny man who was wearing what looked to Mouse like a diaper... and that was all! Mouse was shocked by his almost nakedness but fascinated by the way his legs were intertwined as he sat, posing, on what appeared to be a small, woven mat. Again and again, she'd return to that picture... again and again, she'd attempt to mimic the pose he held... but she could never get all the way there; one of her legs would always pop right out.

She was fascinated, too, by Gypsies. Given a choice at Halloween, she would always choose to dress as a gypsy, so enchanted was she by what she had learned from the Encyclopedia. It was the card reading that so intrigued her. How could they do it? She'd wondered, how could they see someone's future in a bunch of numbers and symbols?

Mouse also became very interested in the planets, a fascination which developed, in her teens, into a passion for astrology. She did not know at the time that she had been blessed with a Scorpionic challenge that had shaped her life as she was born with Chiron sitting on her Scorpio ascendant, the Sun, Moon, Venus, and Jupiter, along with the asteroids Vulcan, Juno, and Ceres all in that first house, all in Scorpio, while Pluto sat at midheaven conjunct Saturn supporting the only-on-planet-Earth events that would become her life.

She very much wanted to take the books upstairs with her to one of the closets where she often hid, so she could be alone while she read and feel more comfortable, but she knew she never could. They were really big books, and it would be a challenge to be discreet about them. Someone would surely notice, and she'd be in trouble. The Encyclopedia was never to be moved from that room.

Mouse had two reading closets, both of them were on the third floor of the house where the live-in help, her horrible uncle—a step-brother of her father—and she had their bedrooms. One of her reading closets was in the hallway, across from the bathroom; the other was in her bedroom. She far preferred the linen closet in the hall as the lighting was better and the piled-up sheets and extra pillows made for more comfortable seating. The closet in the bedroom that she shared with her sisters was tucked into the slope of the roof and had hooks for clothes, but they were unused and, so, a little dangerous when crawling about.

The choice of the closet was a timing thing. The hall closet could be used when most everyone was occupied downstairs, but when there was coming and going happening, the more remote bedroom closet was the logical choice because a person could never be sure about when someone might need a fresh pillowcase.

Mouse didn't think the live-in help would mind finding her in the closet a bit, but she didn't want to burden them with knowing something they ought to, perhaps, report on because she knew they would never want to turn her in. The help were wonderful people, a husband and wife from Haiti. At night, once dinner was over, the kitchen cleaned, and the dishes were done, they would retire to their third-floor room where he—Gilbert—would paint beautiful watercolor scenes of his homeland, and she, Edith, would craft crepe-paper flowers using pipe-cleaners for the stems and stamens.

They were hard workers. Memo even enlisted Gilbert's assistance in burying a limousine in the backyard. Memo had bought the limo on a lark and had found that he far preferred driving his Porsche to being driven and then, for whatever reason, rather than take the limousine to a used car dealer, he buried it. It was odd, but no one dared to ask why. You didn't ask Memo "why" you just did what he told you to do.

Mouse took to visiting Gilbert and Edith once they'd retired for the night. The door to their room was directly across from the top of the stairs and, in the warmer weather, they'd leave the door ajar, thus benefitting from the cross ventilation provided by the open windows in the girls' room down the hall. The aforementioned horrible uncle's room was a very small room to the immediate right of the stairs. He chose to keep his door closed at all times, though he was mostly away at boarding school, which was fine by Mouse. The one and only time he'd invited her into his room to show her some of his books, telling her that he knew how much she loved books, the books he had shown her were so dreadful—and her response so dramatic—that she understood why his door was always closed. She would never understand why it was that he even kept books filled with pictures of dead bodies that (she thought) had obviously starved to death. "Oh, no," he'd evenly explained to her. "Those people were killed in a gas chamber." He'd then gone on to explain how it was that the people had been rounded up, tortured, and sometimes experimented on. Terrified by his seeming enjoyment and sickened by the pictures, she had run down the hall to the bathroom and vomited. After that, she avoided him at all costs.

It was he who noticed her nightly visits to Gilbert and Edith's room and he who informed her father that she was "fraternizing with the help." It was he who got them fired. Mouse was devastated and, for a while, spent an inordinate amount of time in her closets.

Gilbert and Edith were soon replaced by two black women—Mary Truth and Constance Faith—who arrived every morning before Mouse was even awake and left after cleaning up after dinner. They came by bus and would walk down the block—rain or shine—to the house. They left the same way... it wasn't a long walk, only a block, but in snow or rain, it was certainly less than pleasant. One particularly stormy night, thunder and lightning filling the atmosphere with threat, Mouse begged her mother to please, please give Mary Truth, who had stayed late to carry out some extra work, a ride to the corner. Mouse was worried about Mary Truth, whom she'd come to like very much, being so exposed to the lightning.

"She has an umbrella," her mother shot back at her testily. "She'll be fine."

Mouse wanted to grab Mary Truth and hug her, to keep her there, terrified for her life, but Mouse knew what would happen to her if she did... and that Mary Truth might never be allowed to come back at all, so she "sucked it up," as she was so often told to do by her uncle. This was life. This was "the hard truth," as she'd hear people say.

And she'd seen evidence of "hard truth" on television one day when she had "not felt so good" in the morning and had been allowed to stay home from school. Mouse was not overly fond of school and would, as often as seemed prudent, which wasn't nearly enough as far as she was concerned, fake some sort of mild illness. One day, she'd come across a televised live session of the

McCarthy trials and had observed men who reminded her very much of the way her Pop-pop—her mother's father—was. She wouldn't know the words for that till she was older—words like 'arrogant' and 'entitled' and 'mean-spirited'—but she knew that the men she designated as 'bad men', the men who were pummeling the men who were on trial with rapid-fire questions that were designed to bring their integrity into question, were, in fact, bad. She knew good when she saw it and she knew bad when she saw it too. She knew it with every cell in her body.

Mouse had grown to admire Mary Truth, who was one of a group of women—essentially urban slaves—who were referred to as "Father Divine's Angels." Father and Mother Divine, black folk, also owned a massive home in the country. It was easily the size of a hotel but long rather than tall. They supported themselves and their extensive staff by hiring out black women for domestic labor in the Philadelphia area. The Angels always had names like Mary's with some kind of virtuous modifier attached, like Faith or Prudence, names that were pretty obviously not their birth names and were designed to let potential employers know that these were righteous women who would not be given to stealing or laziness and who would be suitable guardians for their children.

For Mouse, the Angels, the ones who came on a regular basis, were people she could trust. She knew that they would not let her get away with things like swimming in the pool without her bathing suit, but she also knew that they'd help her pick out clothes when she had to go shopping with her mother and make sure that she was "presentable" when her parents arrived home after work, because "the last thing anyone wants to see when they get home is a couple of rag-a-muffins in their house."

But Mouse, in addition to being insatiably curious, was also a dreamer and Mary Truth intrigued her. Mary Truth was the tallest person Mouse had ever seen, man or woman, and she was as thin as a rail. She had, in one of her ear lobes, a hole—absolutely, perfectly round and smooth—that was about an eighth of an inch in diameter. Mouse, coming as she did from a house where Cuba had the upper hand, had had her ears pierced for as long as she could remember; she knew that whatever that hole was in Mary Truth's ear, it was no standard piercing... and her imagination ran with that, imagining Mary Truth as a fearless hunter, her ear pierced with some sort of immense golden ring, or fang, stalking prey in the wilds of Africa, running as fast as the wind, always victorious in her quest, the pride of her tribe, an independent woman... maybe even a queen.

One thing she could never figure out, though, was a comment that her mother had made one morning when she was dawdling over her breakfast. Mouse liked the white of the sunny-side-up eggs but not so much the yolk. She generally hoped to be able to make a dash for the trash with her plate while no one was looking. On this particular day, though, her mother happened to walk in just as Mary Truth was reminding Mouse that she needed to eat the yolk and as the Mouse had begun her surreptitious slide away from the table with her plate.

Then, as if out of nowhere, came her mother's voice, "Just because she's brown doesn't mean that you don't have to listen to her. Finish your egg."

Just because she's brown? Mouse thought. She was flummoxed. What on earth could that have to do with anything? She finished her egg as she'd been instructed, but the question remained.

Mommy and Daddy worked at different hospitals, but at both hospitals, there were doctors from all over the world. There was every color of a doctor, all neutral shades, but still... there were definitely brown shades among them. When Mommy and Daddy had parties at home, Mouse would try to mentally match all the different skin colors with those in her crayon box and there were far more shades of brown and grey and black and caramel and puce people than there were crayons in her box.

So it wasn't that brown people couldn't tell you what to do. No, that couldn't be it. There were brown doctors and Mouse presumed that they were probably always telling people what to do, and Mary Truth was always telling her what to do and she did as she was told.

Mouse was very confused.

"Hurry up," said Mommy, ignoring her daughter's question. "You'll be late." Quite a few years would pass before Mouse understood what had gone on that morning when her mother had said, "Just because she's brown," before she would learn that, for some people, money makes a whole lot of things okay that wouldn't otherwise be.

In the evening, Mary Truth and Constance Faith would prepare dinner in that big kitchen that lay at the back of the house. It had a door to the expansive yard that surrounded the house on three sides. There was also a back stairway that led from the second floor right into the kitchen; that was there so "the help" would not be seen using the far more glamorous and wide front stairs. The help cleaned the front stairs, but they did not use them as stairs. Nobody seemed to care what stairs Mouse used—or even, for that matter, where she was—and so, when it was time for making dinner, she'd creep quietly down the back stairs so that she could overhear the casual banter between the two brown women as they prepared dinner while they listened to Amos & Andy on the radio. It was one of the best parts of her day. Amos and Andy were very funny.

Mouse felt lucky in that Mary Truth wasn't required—or didn't feel that she needed to keep a strict eye on Mouse, and she reveled in the small freedom, spending most of her time in closets, reading, or, if the weather was good, either in her private apartment above the garage where her father would meet her sometimes, outside in the pretend log-cabin or hiding in the huge forsythia bush at the far back corner of the property where it joined, but was separated from the arboretum and art museum next door and the nurse's dormitory for the old-age home that spanned most of a block behind the house. The dormitory was as decrepit as the Museum property was fabulous and extravagant. It was constructed of wood and had never been painted, so it was about as dark and spooky and scary as a place could be. Had it not been for the fact that she had seen perfectly healthy-looking young women dressed in immaculate white nurse outfits going in and out of the door every once in a while, she'd have been terrified of the place.

The pretend log cabin in the yard was small and barely held Mouse and Annie at the same time, but when Annie was in the mood, they'd have pretend tea parties there. Mouse wasn't much on pretend. It just seemed kind of dumb; she far preferred reading, but she and Annie were close, and Annie didn't ask for much from anyone, so Mouse gave in on occasion.

She didn't go to the apartment—which was above the three-car garage—much because, mostly, that was just for Daddy and her. But there was a little TV in there and if it was raining, and she couldn't be outside and was bored of being inside, she might go up there and watch TV. The only furniture in the apartment was a bed and the small television, though there was also a cot mattress in the room where the television was, so she could lounge there if she wanted. As little girls go, she enjoyed quite a bit of what seemed freedom to her.

The best spot, though, was the hollow space created by the forsythia bush at the far corner of the yard and the azaleas that nestled into it, creating a very private space where Mouse could spend time with the faeries that she knew were there. Even though her mother made it quite clear that faeries were imaginary beings, Mouse felt otherwise. She could sense their presence and she reveled in it. If Jesus could be real… it just made sense to her that faeries could be real as well.

Mommy had taken her to church a few times, which was where she'd learned about Jesus. She really, really, really did not like church… not the priests, not the lectures, not the kneeling, and she found the whole confession thing to be both creepy and wrong. The Jesus guy, though, him, she liked. She understood him, she thought. You do what you have to do, you endure stuff that seems awful, and you help out when you can. But, like with the faeries, there was no real proof, was there? Still... Jesus seemed possible.

Because of this open-mindedness, perhaps, it was no surprise for her when, one day, as she set foot out of the tiny log cabin, and she heard a voice, as clear as the day, telling her that she should go to her room, gather up all her stuffed animals and dolls, and bring them all out to the front lawn, she did not even pause to question it. She knew, however, that Mary Truth and Constance Faith would most likely object to her toting all her toy friends out to the front lawn. So, she wisely checked the front door to see if it was open since she knew that her guardians were most likely in the kitchen where the back stairs were... but the front stairs were right there, right inside a front door that was used mostly for special guests. Even Mommy and Daddy came and went by the kitchen door because the garage was out back.

The front door was unlocked, and Mouse was in as quietly as the creature she was nicknamed for. She crept up the stairs to her room, gathered up stuffies and dolls alike, and carried them out to the front lawn where the voice had told her to put them. She arranged them all neatly, in two rows, on the slight incline that served to dramatize a three-step walk-up in the brick path that led from the narrow private road on which they lived to the forest green front door with its large brass knocker. She then stepped back to settle herself in the grass, facing her inanimate friends.

"Today is your birthday," the voice reiterated.

Okay, Mouse thought. *This is my real birthday.* She saw no reason to either dispute or question the statement; adults were always making stuff up. This felt correct to her. She sang Happy Birthday to herself and her friends in her head and then returned them all to the bedroom, remaining undetected.

She felt both satisfied and, for some reason, she could never have pinpointed—or even named, for that matter—validated.

A few years or so later, on a visit to Mommy's hair salon, as she sat in the waiting area, reading the horoscope column in a woman's magazine, the woman seated next to her leaned over towards her and commented on the fact that she was, in fact, reading.

"You're reading your horoscope, then, are you?"

Mouse looked up at her and, not really interested in having a conversation, simply answered the woman, "Yes," and went on reading.

The voice interrupted her again. "When were you born?" the woman asked.

Annoyed by the interruption but also knowing that it was not good to be annoyed with grown-ups, she answered, "1946."

Again, the voice, laughing, "No, I meant what month were you born; what day?"

"November," Mouse replied.

"Oh!" the woman exclaimed with seeming delight, "you're a Sagittarius."

"No," Mouse answered. "I'm not."

"Well, if you were born in November," responded the woman, "you most certainly are."

"No," Mouse repeated, just as firmly as she had before. "I'm not."

That was the end of the conversation. Mouse had learned an important lesson. When asked when her birthday was, she now understood that what that signified to most people was "the day your body was born" and that, to avoid future misunderstandings, she would always tell these inquiring people that she had been born in November because she had no way of understanding, let alone explaining, how it was that 'she' and her body had come to Earth on two different days. It was just that way and that was all.

There were lots of things that Mouse had simply learned to accept. One of those things was piano lessons. Why did she need those? Mommy had an organ in the living room, which she loved to play. Mouse had never shown the least bit of interest in it. She wasn't all that crazy about the sounds it made, either. The piano, which was called "a baby grand," was in the part of the basement that had been turned into a bar so Memo and Polly could have a place just for entertaining and drinking. Some of their friends also played piano as well and their parties could be quite lively. They had a friend named Doodles Weaver, whose name fascinated Mouse. He liked to put on a kind of comedy show and play piano at the same time. They all seemed to be having a great time but none of it particularly interested Mouse except as a sort of curious fascination. She would sometimes sit high up on the steps that led from the kitchen to there to watch and listen… till she got noticed. Then she'd be banished to bed.

That was as much interest as she'd ever had in the piano. Yet there she ended up, every afternoon, for half an hour, with a metronome going "practicing." Worse yet, Polly had gotten her a teacher. Happily, though, her interest was so lackadaisical that the teacher resigned, and Mouse was off the hook!

The Accident

School

For some time, Mouse had been overhearing, in bits and pieces, conversations concerning herself and school. She dreaded going to school. Not in an 'afraid' sort of way; she saw it, rather, as an imposition on her time and freedom. The reality of it turned out to be every bit as dreadful as her projections... worse, actually... at first, it was mostly the uniforms.

The school that Mommy had in mind for her was a Catholic school which Mouse imagined might be every bit as irritating as church had been: lots of pompous grown-ups talking about "sin." She was prepared for that mental intrusion. But the itching instigated by the edges of the wool bolero and skirt that she was required to wear just about drove her mad. There was no moment, despite wearing the slip that Mommy had said would help, that Mouse was not being driven almost mad from itching because, of course, she could not be seen scratching. That was unseemly... unfeminine.

It was even worse in the second year when Annie had to go too, as Annie seemed not the least bit affected by either ideology or itching, which made Mouse look as if she were just "a complainer." Mommy was pregnant again, still working full time, and she had no time for Mouse's "nonsense," but at some point, Mommy and Daddy decided together that the private school—and Mouse hadn't even known that it was "private" whatever that meant—was going to be too much of an expense what with another child coming so Mouse and Annie would be transferred the following year to a "parochial" school.

"Parochial," was that even a real word? Mouse wondered. She'd never heard it before and had the devil of a time trying to look it up. Pah-rO-kial ? Pu-rO-quial ? Only stumbling across the word "orcha" one day when she was reading about whales had allowed her to expand her spelling option possibilities to the degree required in order to determine that, essentially, she'd be going to Catholic school again. She hoped the uniforms might not be quite as itchy... and they weren't.

But they weren't not itchy either. Still, by comparison, they were tolerable. The fabric was a lighter weight and so cooler, at least. And that was good because, unlike the private school, which had sent a small bus-sort-of vehicle to pick up the students, everybody that went to the parochial school either walked to get there or got dropped off by their parents. Most of the students lived within a few blocks of the school, but Mouse and Annie lived about half a mile away and had to cross one major street that was not regulated with either a traffic light or a stop sign. Mouse and Bug—which was Annie's 'family' name—would be walking as Mommy had to leave for work much earlier than school opened.

The private road they were living on that led past the fabulously large arboretum next door to their house was just that—a road. There were no sidewalks. The arboretum was bounded on all sides by the same wrought iron fence that defined the side of their lawn at home. The entrance to the property itself, though, was guarded by a double gate that opened from the middle but was almost always closed. The gate was monitored by three Doberman dogs that flew up, barking and growling and showing their teeth at anyone who passed by on foot. It was not something that either of the girls ever got used to; it terrified them every day, but the only alternate way home was much longer and required that they first walk away from the school—and their home—toward the center of town, to a sidewalk that ran along a main four-lane highway carrying busses and trucks. It was loud and a little scary and it smelled terrible, so they tolerated the Doberman fright, knowing, if only intellectually, that they were safe. But everything changed early that summer.

Mouse and Bug had a playset in the back yard, close to the play log cabin; it was an all-in-one-piece set, the sort that was designed for use by small children, which, of course, they were, but their next-door neighbors, who had kids older than they were, had a for-real playground-quality sliding-board and swing set. Their son was only a couple of years older than Mouse and she often played ball with him and the other boys that lived down the street… that was part of the street that led to the big road where the busses came and went. There were no girls their age in the neighborhood and so the only 'play' options, aside from dolls and each other, were boys' games, which Annie eschewed. Mouse liked the boys more than she liked the games and they seemed to know that, so they always let her play.

Melvin's family, who lived in the house that was right next door, ate dinner much earlier than Mouse's family, partially because her parents always had "cocktail hour" before dinner. One evening, during cocktail hour, Mouse convinced Annie to come out and play on the slide... but not the usual way. Mouse had found that just climbing up and sliding down, over and over and over again, was deadly boring. What she liked to do was to stand under the sliding board, walk to the place where she could reach up and just about grab the rounded metal railings on either side. Then, like the monkeys she'd seen at the zoo, she'd reach back as far as she could, grabbing the railing and pulling her body off the ground just an inch or so, just enough to be able to swing herself—like a monkey—far enough to be able to grab the railing on the other side with her free hand... at that point her toes would be just skimming the ground. She would then continue to swing her body from side to side, as if she were a pendulum, using the momentum generated by the previous swing, and she would gradually get her swinging body higher and higher up the sliding board till her feet were way off the ground. When she got to the highest point, where the slide connected with the top of the ladder, she'd let go and drop to the ground.

Mouse demonstrated her trick to Annie and called Annie to try it with her, which Annie did, falling in place behind Mouse so that she could follow her moves, which she did. This positioning placed her higher up on the underside. In just moments, they were both swinging free and mere seconds later, the momentum they had generated pulled the large spikes that had been holding the sliding board to the ground out of the ground, and the slide, rather than rocking in place, as it had been, began to follow its side-to-side momentum. With each swing, the slide was moving a little more and getting a little closer to the ground each time; it was on an inevitable crash course.

Mouse finally felt the slide's growing momentum and its downward trend and reached back to grab Annie by the arm so that she could pull them both out the open side, but Annie, who never liked to be told what to do, pulled herself free from Mouse's grasp, and, falling outward, was struck on the side of her head by the plummeting slide, and pushed to the ground, her skull crushed under its weight. Mouse ran immediately to the opposite side, where Annie lay, with the sliding board, pinning her head to the ground. Annie's eyes were closed. There was blood everywhere.

Knowing that there was nothing she could do—the sliding board was huge and heavy—Mouse ran as fast as she could, across the neighbor's yard, through the sticker-bush hedge, past the huge garage at the end of their driveway and up the path to the back door. The screen door was open and she crashed through, startling Mary Truth and Constance Faith, who stood at the stove and sink, preparing for dinner. They called after her to slow down as they saw that she was headed for the cellar stairs, which led to the bar downstairs, where she knew she would find her parents having their pre-prandial cocktails.

"The sliding board fell on Annie!" she cried out halfway down the stairs, "...and her nose is bleeding."

Her parents moved faster than she had ever seen either of them move, but she was right behind them.

Tracing the very same path she'd taken, they ran to the neighbor's yard. Daddy—who lifted weights every morning—yanked the sliding board up as high as he could, freeing his now comatose daughter. Polly dragged Annie out as Memo let the slide drop to the ground. He then swooped Annie up in his arms and started shouting directions to Mommy. "Get towels, rags, anything," he cried out. Polly ran and returned in what seemed like seconds, her arms filled with dinner napkins and towels.

"Get in the car," he said. "No!" he cried out as she headed for the driver's seat.

She knew immediately that, of course, he would drive. His hobby was race car driving; now, he'd put his experience on the track to a profound test. Polly got into the passenger seat and he carefully placed their bleeding daughter on her lap, helping Polly to rotate herself and her limp child far enough into the car that he could shut the door, but before he shut it, he swabbed Annie's face with one of the linen napkins, rolled down the car window a little and tucked the bloody rag into the opening. He then rolled the window back up again, creating a dreadful-looking rag/flag sure to catch the eye of anyone questioning the driving he intended to do. And then they were gone.

By that time, Mary Truth had come out of the house. She'd kept her distance from the action but moved in quickly to swoop up Mouse and take her inside, where she offered her what comfort she could. No one ate the dinner that had been prepared and Mary Truth never left that night. Nor did Mommy and Daddy come home.

The next day, when they did come home, they told Mouse that Annie was "okay" but that she was going to be staying in the hospital for a while and since it was summer and school was a long way off, they told her they thought that she—the Mouse—should spend the summer with family friends of theirs in a place called Stone Harbor, a seashore resort in New Jersey. Mouse knew their friends, they had a son that was a little older than she was and a daughter who was the same age as Annie. Their mother was a doctor too. But Mouse didn't want to go. She wanted to stay home. She wanted to know what was going on. She wanted to be able to visit Annie in the hospital. She knew you could do that, but that Friday, her mother packed her bags and drove her to Stone Harbor. She spent the summer there and did the things that everyone there was doing, like going to the beach and the boardwalk, but it was, to her, as if she was in a kind of trance. By the time the end of August rolled around and it was time to go home, Mouse couldn't even remember how she had spent her time. There was only one thing she did remember and that was the sight of the older brother's penis not-quite-visible under a soaking wet white T-shirt and underpants that he'd worn into the outdoor shower one day. That, for whatever reason, she would end up being able to vividly recall until she was a very old woman.

Time lost all meaning for Mouse that summer. While it seemed as if it would never end, when her mother finally did come to pick her up in late August, it almost seemed as if the summer had never happened. To her great relief, before her mother drove her home, she took her to the hospital where Annie was staying. She had been there all summer. Mommy said that maybe soon when she woke up, she would come home.

Mouse didn't understand. When she woke up? Woke up? She's been asleep all this time?

Her mother explained that Anne had sort of 'fallen asleep' when her skull had been crushed and that she just hadn't stopped sleeping yet, but when Mouse got there, to the room in the hospital where her sister lay, she was horrified. Annie wasn't "sleeping"... she was hooked up to some machine and there were tubes coming out of her, some of them out of her head! Mouse couldn't stay; she ran from the room and waited outside, so overwrought that she didn't even try to hear what Mommy and the other doctors were saying.

"It's okay, Mouse. She's okay. She'll be okay."

It sure didn't look that way to Mouse.

Back to School

Mouse was and would remain throughout her life—a devoted fan of Peanut Butter. It was her favorite snack... but, knowing that it was her favorite snack, the help generally placed it where she couldn't reach it because, spoon in hand, she would go for it throughout the day. One day, craving peanut butter, she went on a search, finding it about three shelves out of her reach in a free-standing metal cabinet that was usually reserved for canned goods.

Stretching her arm up as far as she could, she could... just... about... but... not... quite... No! Darn, she thought to herself, stepping back to assess her options. The option she decided upon was to climb the shelves until she could reach it. Seeing no one nearby, she reached up to clutch the edge of the shelf, first with one hand, then the other, then, tentatively lifting her left foot from the floor, she began to pull herself up... and... the cabinet rocked forward. It all happened so fast that there was no chance of escape, and there she lay, on the floor, with a metal cabinet and all of its contents on top of her, pinned down which no hope of escape.

Needless to say, the calamitous noise did not go unnoticed and before she even had time to think about how she might extricate herself, there they were, standing over her, Mary Truth and Constance Faith with looks on their faces such as she had never seen and hoped never to see again. She was briefly sentenced to "sit there" and watch them work together to clean up and put everything back in order.

Oddly, Mouse didn't have a bruise on her, and she was confident that neither of her caretakers would say anything about the incident to her parents and they were fairly confident that Mouse would not be scaling any kitchen furniture in the near future. Still, school would be a welcome respite for them all.

School started up once September rolled around and even though Annie wasn't home yet, at least things started to seem a little more normal.

Mouse, as shy as she was, felt like an outsider in this new school, not that she'd ever made any friends in the private school, but she'd gotten used to it there. When it came time for recess when the weather was good, all the students went outside to the large asphalt "playground," where there were a couple of basketball nets hung low so that elementary school students could easily make baskets, but that was about all there was. The girls tended to play circle games which involved, as a rule, holding hands, forming a large circle, and rotating around. Mouse was never invited to play and so she generally spent her free time lounging on the iron fire-escape steps just outside the double doors that led to the auditorium, from which vantage point she would scan the large, old trees that grew in the backyards of surrounding homes.

She was intrigued by the growths on many of the trees, large bulges that she imagined were the hardened-over bottoms of other children who, like her, had escaped from their bodies to 'hide' inside the trees, while below, men were sticking their big hard penises into them. *Those children in trees, though,* she thought, *they must have gotten stuck inside the trees... or maybe they just didn't want to come out again.*

She hadn't been scared at all when it had happened to her when the men put their penises in her. As if she knew exactly what she was doing, she had sort of popped out of her body and then swam into the roots of the first tree she came across and the next thing she knew, she would be sitting on a branch of the tree, high above her own body yet somehow in touch with it. The tree would be telling her what to do in order to make the man not hurt her and get off of her more quickly and somehow, down there, in the woods, her body was doing what the tree was telling her to do. One by one, men put their penises in her and then went away and then it was over.

Annie couldn't do what she could do, though. She couldn't seem to get out of her body. She hated what was happening to her and so because she tried to fight off the men who were taking turns invading her small body, she got tied down... then she got tied up before getting put in the trunk of her grandfather's car for the ride back to their grandparents' house.

Despite spending most of the provided recess time after lunch sitting alone on the iron fire escape steps and fantasizing about the unfortunate children she imagined stuck in the trees, Mouse made a friend. Her name was Marie. The first part of Marie's walk home happened to be the first part of a way that Mouse could go if she wanted a change of scenery and without Annie to have to answer to, she was free to do just that, and she did. This slight adjustment meant that she could walk almost halfway home with her friend who, one day, invited her in and, for whatever reason, showed her a secret, pulling off her uniform, then opening up her blouse to reveal the fact that she had three nipples.

Mouse was speechless and also a little scared. She didn't know why she was scared; she just was. She returned to her usual route home and that was the end of that friendship. But she had Annie now, back at home, and a whole new window on the world was opened for her as a result.

Annie was in bed most of the time as she was unable to walk. In the morning, Daddy would carry Annie from their shared bedroom to the big bedroom where he and Mommy slept at night so that she could watch television during the day. When Mouse arrived home, she'd join her there and together, they would watch American Bandstand. It was okay with Annie because, it seemed, almost anything was. She didn't say much, and what she did say was difficult to understand.

Mouse loved the music and would bounce around on the floor pretending to dance like she always wanted to when there were bands playing on the Ed Sullivan shows on Sunday nights, but she was embarrassed to do that because her parents were there and they were both good dancers. Sometimes Annie's special nurse would show up in the afternoon to check on her. She was a beautiful dark-skinned woman named Addie. She was strong, and she would lift Annie out of bed, pivoting her onto a wheelchair so that she could take her outside for a while, which was easy because there was a second-floor porch right outside the room that overlooked the backyard and the arboretum next door.

A New Year's Day to Remember

When New Year's Eve rolled around that year, Polly and Memo received an invitation to a New Year's Day party "they couldn't refuse." But what to do with the girls? It was a holiday; there was no 'help' available on holidays, so Polly went the extra mile, contacting the staff that oversaw Father Divine's Angels to see if there was any way that they would consider "taking the girls in," just for a few hours. Money is so often a dependable changer of minds and policies.

The Angels—all, save for the ones that worked at Father Divine's Estate—lived in an historical hotel on North Broad Street, not far from City Hall, that was built of yellow Pompeian brick. It had originally been The Lorraine Hotel, but when Father Divine purchased it as housing for his tribe of Angels, it had been re-named The Divine Lorraine Hotel. Here it was, that Mouse and

Annie spent New Year's Day afternoon and evening among the Angels who paid them "no mind at all," going about their day as if it were no different from any other day.

The place was grand inside, like nothing either of the girls had ever seen before, with dark woodwork and carvings and an elaborate window seat on the second floor, which was where they spent their time. A few hours in, though, Mouse started to smell something funny... unpleasant, she thought, really. It turned out to be their dinner.

The dinner was served in the basement, in a long room that was connected to the kitchen where she imagined it had been prepared. The stairway down—also of dark wood—was very, very narrow, like the back stairs at home. But there were photographs lining the walls and as the parade of Angels was moving quite slowly, Mouse had the opportunity to inspect the pictures closely. Most of them were of The Divine Family, their suburban mansion that resembled two or three motels stuck together, and the staff that cared for all of that. Mouse was astounded; it was the longest house she'd ever seen. She would not have been surprised if it had been a hotel, but it wasn't. It was their home. It was two—or maybe three stories high, she couldn't tell for sure. The staff was lined up in front of it, with Father and Mother Divine front and center. The line ran almost the entire length of the edifice.

Mouse didn't know what to think. Here she was, with the Angels, in a place that had once been considered fancy but was now dark and old and overcrowded, "celebrating" in a basement that smelled more like old urine than any kind of dinner. How could those people in the picture live with themselves? How could they be all rich and fancy and living in a castle while all these women were living like college students but in a dark dormitory? She was angry. It was unfair. And what could she do about it? Nothing. She couldn't even tell her parents because they would tell her that it was really just fine and that the Angels were fortunate to have work and a place to stay.

A Trip to the Mountains

Every year Polly and Memo would take a trip to a resort in the Pocono Mountains to celebrate their wedding anniversary. The year after Annie's accident, though, they decided to take Annie and Mouse along, too, as a special treat. They wheeled Annie on all the trails around the resort as Mouse tagged along behind. At one point, a family coming towards them from the other direction had to pass very close to them on the trail and as they walked by, one of their children called out, "Hey, Mommy, how come that boy has a dress on?"

Annie's hair was longer than it had been, but it was still in a sort of crewcut, and her face was still paralyzed on one side following the surgeries she'd had. Annie was clearly embarrassed by the comment, but Mouse was angry. "She's a girl, stupid," Mouse wanted to shout out, but she knew she'd get in trouble for that, so she swallowed the words before they got out of her mouth.

Mouse watched as Mommy calmly informed the child, and the parents, that Annie'd had a bad accident and an operation and that they'd had to shave her hair for the surgery.

It was better at home, Mouse decided. Easier. Fewer people stared.

Something had happened, though, between Mouse and Annie. Maybe it had been the result of so much time spent apart. Maybe it was just that Annie had changed because she had, though Mouse couldn't put her finger on what had changed exactly. The bond they'd had, cemented by enduring the awful events in the woods together, with Mouse calming Annie down afterward, soothing her... it seemed to have all disappeared and slowly, even though they shared a bedroom, they began to grow apart.

Dancing & Art Classes

No doubt influenced by her own father's child-rearing techniques, Mommy began directing the course of Mouse's life in the direction she felt that it should go. The first thing on her list was ballet lessons. This thought may have been based on the Mouse's total inability to stay still when any kind of music was on. It was impossible to ignore her gyrations in response to any kind of dancing on television. The Whirling Dervishes on the Ed Sullivan Show set her to spinning, while the Rock'n'Roll bands had her begging for 45s and her own record player. The usual answer to "Where's the Mouse now?" was most likely, "In the sunroom!"

The sunroom had never gotten much use until the Mouse took to dancing. It was a wonderful room, with a black and white checkerboard tiled floor, perfect for dance play. She'd always beg to go along when Mommy went shopping and would use her meager allowance to pick up 45s whenever the opportunity presented itself. She didn't have a large selection of music, but she had curated it perfectly to suit her need to dance like a leaf in the wind.

Of course, though, every well-trained young lady needs ballet lessons and so, ballet lessons it was... every Saturday morning for what seemed like an eternity to Mouse.

The lessons were frustrating for her and although she didn't realize it at the time, they were also the first indication of her left-right confusion.

The teacher would give an instruction such as, "Left foot forward, right arm up," and there Mouse would be, always a couple of seconds late because she didn't know... she couldn't know... and she would always end up at least one beat behind everyone else, her body making tentative starts because her body didn't know right from left either. Eventually, over time, Mouse would begin to associate that her "right" hand was the hand with the thumb that had the big scar on it from the earlier incident with the tin can in the garage, but there would always have to be time for an internal mental adjustment to be made.

Mouse, though, hated the classes not only because of her embarrassment but because it wore her out to be that mentally "on call" while dancing, an activity that she knew as one of total freedom from thought. Happily, though, it was that very challenge that got her out of having to take the classes. At the end of the school year, each class put on a performance for the parents. Every child in the class participated. Mouse had been given a smaller role than any of the others, for which she was grateful, but she still had to be on a stage, performing in front of a real audience. She was scared but not frozen in fear when she stepped out from the curtain in order to perform a movement known as a 'degage.' The movement, which looks a bit like a fancy, toe-pointed small kick, was to have been performed with her right leg... it got performed, though, with her left and, in so doing, took out a critically placed piece of scenery which toppled over, taking out most of the scenery on that side of the stage.

The audience loved it. The ballet teacher was definitely not happy. Mouse was devastated by embarrassment, but in the end, it was worth it. Her days in ballet class were over, but her mother's quest for Mouse to do whatever it was that she was supposed to be doing was not over and directly on the heels of the ballet fiasco had come the art lessons.

The art lessons were held on Saturdays at the Philadelphia Museum of Art. By now, with a few children under their belts, though, Mommy and Daddy had taken to spending a few weekends a month away from their responsibilities by going to Ocean City, where they'd purchased a house on the bay so that Daddy could have a boat. Consequently, Mouse was required to take the bus in and out of town. She was old enough, Mommy told her, as she walked and rode with her through a trip there and back, and the bus stopped right at the end of their street. That's where Mary Truth and Constance Faith got the bus and if they could do it, so could she. But they're grown-ups, thought Mouse, not speaking her thoughts aloud.

Art lessons were better than ballet, at least. Tolerable, but she didn't love them. What she did love, though, was the museum itself and discovering that "art" could mean anything from painting and drawing to assemblages of metal and glass and wood. Since she was on her own, after class, she could wander as she pleased.

Over time, she developed favorites, two of which she would visit every week.

The first of the two was an immense painting, so large that it had its own room. Its title was Prometheus Bound. The painting showed a young man, naked save for a narrow white swath of cloth that had been strategically placed so as to obscure his genitals. A huge eagle had opened a wound just below his ribcage and was laboring to remove his liver.

She read the story that accompanied the work. It was a myth. She was glad to know that part, but she knew people; she'd been in the woods where very bad things happened, so the mere fact that some painter had pictured a man being punished in this inhuman way proved to her that human men could think horrible things and paint them to show people: "this is the awful thing I thought!" It almost seemed to make it okay… if it's okay to think, then maybe it's okay to do.

The story said that the event pictured happened over and over again every day. Yes, she'd think to herself. It probably does... something like it... somewhere, to someone.

The painting captured every ounce of her attention. Other viewers would come and go, seemingly oblivious to her small presence there.

That was how she felt... like that man in the picture... as if she had no say in what happened to her in her life and some of it had been pretty awful. Somehow, the fact of his pain and helplessness, and the fact that at least someone had noticed, that someone had shown it to the world, gave her a strange kind of hope.

The other painting was almost around the corner from the first. It was a simple, straightforward seated portrait of a young Spanish nobleman. The young man was in a sideways presentation and totally naked. His skin was the whitest skin that Mouse had ever seen. Mouse's skin was a color that her mother called "olive" in the wintertime, but for most of the year, it was tanned from the sun, and she looked every bit the Cuban that her father was. She was riveted by the young Spaniard in the painting, his nakedness and snow-white skin making him look utterly vulnerable. There was something about the look in his eyes that seemed to say to her, "I don't want to be here, doing this."

The painting fascinated her. He was not tied to the chair, as Prometheus was tied to the rock, but it was clear—if only to her—that he was very, very uncomfortable. And that skin... so white... he looked as if he had been drained of all his blood... maybe he had.

Decades later, as an adult, she would visit the paintings again... and feel exactly the same way.

Play Farm Day Camp

Mommy had a special treat for her girls that summer… something called "day camp." Mouse had no idea what that meant but discovered that the first thing it meant was that she and Annie were going to get dropped off at the home of one of the doctors that her mother worked with, the doctor whose son she had been so fascinated by in a previous summer when she'd stayed with them at the shore while Annie was in the hospital. Mouse didn't mind that idea at all but was disappointed to discover that the boy would not be attending camp with them. Still, she got to see him at the house, and that was something.

The reason for the drop-off was that the camp had its own little bus that went around and picked up all the camp-goers in that area. The bus didn't travel to where Mouse lived, so they had to go to Mommy's friend's house. At first, nobody knew anybody on the bus, but as the summer wore on, they all got to be friendly and would often play word games or have contests trying to recite all the names of the foreign kids—which Mouse and Annie got lumped into because of their 'extra' names—the result of having been confirmed in the Catholic Church—and their Spanish-sounding last name. Mouse had fun correcting them.

They'd play lots of games at camp, including Mouse's favorite, called Red Rover, which was a game where everyone in the group, but one, lined up in a row facing one kid across from them. Each child in the line was to silently pick a color and hold that in mind. The task of the one kid task standing alone across from them was to shout out the command "Red Rover, Red Rover for—whatever color he or she would choose—to come over." If that happened to be the color that you had picked, then you had to go over to stand behind the caller.

If there was a child whose color was never called, that was the winner. Mouse won so many times that they just stopped playing the game. She had the BIG box of crayons at home. She knew "burnt umber" and "raw sienna" and numerous other obtuse colors.

On the last day of camp, though, Mouse got her comeuppance. The last day was given to all sorts of games and a lot of swimming contests. As the day was winding down, and everyone had been gathered around the swimming pool, a break for a bit of a nap was announced and the campers were instructed to spread out their towels, lie down, and close their eyes for a little bit of a rest. All of the campers, Mouse included, did as instructed.

The next thing that the napping Mouse heard were the words, "Take off your wet suits..." so she rose to a standing position and pulled her suit down. It was around her ankles, and she was about to step out of it when she fully regained consciousness and everyone—every child, at any rate—was laughing hilariously. She had never been so embarrassed.

She did not speak another word to anyone there, not even on the way home. If she could have disappeared into nothingness, she would have. She would not return the following year. It would be decades before she realized that she'd been unconsciously following directions just as she'd been taught to do by her father and by her grandfather. Don't ask questions; just do what you are told to do.

One Last Time

Mouse's heart sank when she saw her mother's car parked in front of the school one Friday afternoon. Whatever she was there for, it couldn't be good. She never left work in the middle of the day. Mouse turned to look back to see if Annie, who was able to walk on her own again, had gotten out of class. She'd missed a year and was now in a new group of classmates. More shy, even, than Mouse, Annie had made no new friends yet. Mouse could see her approaching slowly with her slightly askew gait.

Polly leaned across the broad front seat of the wood-paneled station wagon, rolled down the window, and signaled Mouse to get in the back seat. They waited for Annie to arrive and as they took off, she explained that she was taking them to the train station in center-city where she was going to put them on the train for

Reading, where Nana and Pop-Pop would meet them to take them for the weekend.

That could only mean one thing. Mouse's heart sank. It was going to happen again, the horrible smells and the men, and the blood... and Annie... oh. But there was nothing to be done; there were no words that could be spoken, not if she valued their lives.

Mouse never really liked going into the city. She far preferred the backyard and the gardens at home. Mommy parked the car in some huge place that was very dark and filled with the smell of exhaust and something else unpleasant. She took Mouse by the hand, telling her to take Annie's hand and "Don't let go!" and they rushed off to the place where the train was waiting, its engine running and looking as if it were already filled with passengers.

A woman in what looked like a policeman's uniform came out and approached Polly and the girls; she'd obviously been informed about these particular passengers. After a quick reassurance to the girls, Polly handed them over to the stewardess and waved them off. The stewardess took off at a decent clip as the girls walked as fast as they could to keep up with her. She settled them into the outer two seats of a set of three, the window seat having already been occupied by an older man... an older man that Mouse, now seated right next to him, thought she recognized from the woods. She felt frozen in place.

Not too long after the train got underway, the stewardess came around wearing a tray that was suspended by a strap that went up and around the back of her neck. The tray was laden with treats to offer the passengers... for a price. Mommy hadn't given the girls any money, so all they could do was look longingly at what was on offer.

The man who sat by the window noticed. He waved his hand to catch the attention of the treat-bearer and purchased two chocolate bars and a peanut bar. Leaning across Mouse, he attempted to give Annie a chocolate bar which she eagerly grabbed. He then attempted to give the other one to Mouse; she pushed it away. He began cajoling her so vigorously that she grabbed it from his hand just so he'd stop talking... but she refused to open it and as she sat there, stewing, it melted in her hands. She didn't care.

The train ride was dreadful, noisy, and rickety, bouncing them around in their seats which felt as if they were made from burlap and were, despite appearing to be padded, as uncomfortable as church pews.

Forty minutes or so into the trip, the stewardess came by again and, seeing the mess on Mouse's hands, gave her numerous paper napkins so that she could clean herself up, mentioning something about looking tidy for her grandparents. Then, from the far end of the train, there came an announcement for a stop. It wasn't the Reading stop, where they were supposed to get off, but it was a place name that Mouse recognized.

The man next to her said, as if she were interested, that the next stop was his stop and that he knew where their grandfather lived and would be happy to take them there. His words pressed every "DANGER" button that Mouse had inside her. She managed a curt but polite "No, thank you" as she tried to backhand swat Annie who was in the midst of a clearly rising enthusiasm for getting off the rattletrap of a train.

Mouse already knew what they were in for and while it wasn't good, at least it would be over at some point.

She could only imagine what this horrible, creepy man might have in mind for them. She got a bad feeling from him, and she knew to honor that. She'd never been wrong with her feelings. The rest of the weekend went just as she'd imagined it would.

A little while after dinner, Nana made them a wonderful warm vanilla drink that was laced with something that rendered them both not so much sleepy as kind of limp. Pop-Pop carried Mouse to the car and lay her in the backseat, going back for Annie, who was wriggling more than a little. He didn't like that and called Nana to come out and open the trunk, which she did. He put Annie into the trunk and slammed it shut. Mouse could hear Annie whimpering and after Pop-Pop got the car going, she began to use her fingernails to make scratchy noises on the back of the seat just so that Annie would know that she was there.

Once they'd reached the venue in the woods—the very same place they'd been taken before—Pop-Pop carried the now very limp Mouse over to a grassy spot where he sat her down, going back for Annie, who was at least a little more 'relaxed' as he put it when he dropped her next to her sister. He then walked away some distance to where there were other men and, as Mouse could smell, there was also a fire going.

It was going to be just the same, she thought, only it wasn't. They didn't come for them right away. There were all kinds of yelps and hoots and noises coming from the area where the fire was and then a smell tinged the smoke… it was something like the smell from their neighbors' bar-b-que but not quite.

After the celebratory noises calmed down, the men came for her and Annie and took them to the solid wooden bench-like things that looked as if they had been made out of a tree sawn down the middle. They lay Annie on one and tied her arms down to the bench and then did the same to her. They spread their legs as well and tied them down tight too. It wasn't horribly tight, but it wasn't anything they could break free from… nor did Mouse have any thoughts of trying. She would do the same thing she'd done before, dive out of her body and swim through the earth to the closest tree. Then she'd go up to a good branch—one from which she could see her body below—and talk to herself, calming herself down and sometimes—when she felt as if she were getting a message from somewhere in her body—

tell herself when to wiggle a little. That seemed to help get the men off of her a little faster.

When it was all over, Pop-Pop and another man carried them back to the car, placing Mouse in the backseat as before and almost throwing Annie in the trunk. Mouse gasped at the sound of her sister's body hitting the metal and the groan she couldn't suppress.

"Shaddup," said someone, slamming the trunk lid, leaving Annie alone in the darkness.

On the trip home, Mouse tried scratching on the back seat again, hoping to reassure her sister that she was there. Then she fell back on the seat and watched the stars through the back window as they were transported back to the little house in the woods. She loved the stars and the planets and didn't often have the opportunity to just lie back and look at them.

Back at the house, the girls were carried into the room where they would sleep. Their grandfather was a hoarder of sorts but a very specific kind of hoarder; he kept newspapers and magazines. He had an entire room of the house filled with stacks of them. In the midst of that were placed a wooden desk and two cots where the girls' bodies, limp with drugs and trauma, were set down for the night. In the morning, after breakfast, Nana and Pop-Pop drove them home.

Christmas

Most kids got all hyped up about Christmas, but for Mouse, Christmas meant that in addition to getting a bunch of stuff she mostly didn't care about, Pop-Pop and Nana came to "spend the holiday."

For Mouse, the best thing about the holiday was the postcard that came from "Uncle Jack," usually the week before. Mouse had no idea who Uncle Jack was. No one ever talked about him; he never came to visit, though his Christmas postcard was always displayed along with the rest of the cards from which she understood that, whoever he was, he was "OK" except that he clearly wasn't entirely okay because the handwriting on his postcards was very, very strange... all jagged. You could *read* it but not without effort.

If there was one word that a person could have said defined the Mouse, it would have been 'curiosity.' From her addiction to the Encyclopedia to her utter inability to abide not knowing something, no matter how embarrassing it might prove to the adults around, Mouse WANTED TO KNOW. Not that she'd necessarily remember… but she had to find out.

Polly did not seem at all put off about most of Mouse's questions and was skillful at deflecting the others, but she did not even hesitate to answer Uncle Jack's question. It was something called Parkinson's disease, she told her. It makes people's hands shake. Every year, Mouse looked forward to the postcard from Uncle Jack. It was the effort she knew that he must have put into it and the insistence on doing it that impressed her. She had never met him, but she admired him. And his card was the best part of her Christmas.

Polly had special Christmas stockings made for each of her kids. The stockings were large, much wider and deeper than regular socks, and were made of plush velveteen fabric, red with a white cuff. Each child had their name written on the cuff. Every year, without fail, Pop-Pop would bring a big, old, oversized sock of his own and tack it on to the end of the line of stockings that were all "hung by the chimney with care." Polly always put a potato in it. And every Christmas night, Mouse and Annie, after being ready for bed, were required to go back downstairs in order to say good night to Nana and Pop-Pop.

One Christmas eve, after Mouse and Annie had been all tucked into bed, Mouse got the idea, once she'd seen her parents head off to their bedroom, and heard everything get quiet downstairs, that she'd sneak down the stairs just far enough that Santa couldn't see her and that she'd stay there till she got to see her stocking get filled.

As quietly as she could, she slipped out of bed and made her way silently down the stairs. She spotted Santa... well, the edges of him, his arms kind of poured over the arms of the large, upholstered wing chair that had it's back to the wide opening of the living-room. She froze.

Her heart was pounding. As quietly as she could, she snuck down even farther. She heard snoring! Santa was sleeping! She could sneak around and get a good look. The stockings, she could see, had already been filled, and the scotch in the glass that her mother always left out for him was empty! She determined to go for it and crept, as softly as an actual mouse, down the last few stairs and around the corner. On tip-toe, she approached the back of the chair and cautiously, ever so cautiously, edged toward the front of the chair only to discover... Pop-pop!!!

Her evil grandfather! She was horrified, but she was also terrified of being caught. Maintaining stealth mode to the best of her young ability while, at the same time wanting to run away as fast as she could, she crept away and up the stairs without ever looking back, disillusioned for a lifetime.

A Trip to Cuba

It was decided that Mouse and Annie should take a trip to Havana. Why it had been decided, Mouse would never know. "Mama" (which was pronounced with the emphasis on the second syllable), which is what their father's mother wished to be called, had come to visit them in Philadelphia a couple of years previously and, as she had no desire to learn English, they hadn't really had much to do with each other. Mama was a Rubenesque woman who was never seen without everything about her in perfect order, from her ebony sculptured hair to her high-heeled shoes.

Daddy had stayed home "to hold down the fort" while Mommy accompanied the girls to Havana. It was the first time Mouse would recall going to Cuba. She'd heard that she'd been there when she was a baby, but she didn't remember that. The trip felt like it took forever.

The train ride from Philadelphia to Miami, in their own special room next to Mommy's, was a little more exciting than any of them had imagined as, on the overnight part, the train had gone right next to some huge building that was on fire. The closeness and intensity of the light from the flames had awakened Mouse and terrified her. She was, after all, helpless. The moment the danger had clearly passed, she fell asleep in seconds, exhausted from fear. The airport in Miami had been crowded and noisy and Annie had been clinging to her the whole time. The airplane ride had been kind of scary... and so, at the airport, was Mama, seeming even more imposing than she had remembered her.

Mama's house was nothing like any house Mouse had ever seen. For one thing, the floors were marble. Marble was everywhere, not just in the bathrooms where even the walls were gigantic, solid slabs of it! And, oddly, from Mouse's point of view, there were no windows at all in the bathrooms. All the windows everywhere else had black iron bars on them, kind of like the fence outside the house on Lapsley Lane. Worst of all, though, Mouse wasn't allowed in the kitchen! Ever. No snacks! It all seemed terrible.

That afternoon, though, Mama had what seemed like a fun idea: an early evening dinner picnic. Feeling kind of smothered by the formality of... well... everything about everything, Mouse enthusiastically agreed that she thought that it would be a wonderful plan.

The picnic, though, was nothing like she would have had at home. To begin with, the picnic basket was prepared by the kitchen staff in the kitchen that she wasn't allowed to go into, so she didn't even know what there'd be to eat. No one had asked her or Annie what they liked, but still, it would be a picnic and it would be outside, and outside was just about her favorite place to be and almost anyplace seemed better than the marble jail she was in.

"Outside" turned out to be a vast lawn that fronted two large, square-ish buildings, one of which had a rooftop porch. It didn't seem to Mouse as if it were even a place where you'd be allowed to *have* a picnic. It wasn't a hotel; she could see that. There were no signs anywhere. It reminded her of a hospital, but there wasn't much traffic on the narrow road they'd followed, nor anyplace that looked like a parking lot. But the chauffer and his assistant lay out the blanket that had been brought and toted the baskets from the car, returning to the limo, no doubt for a nap.

Mama and Mommy laid out the small feast and served the girls their idea of an appropriate amount of food for them. As dusk began to fall and a full moon rose, lights came on here and there in the building and the occasional silhouette could be seen passing by a window. It looked to Mouse as if there were children in the smaller building. Then a back-lit dark shape appeared on the rooftop porch of the larger building. It looked like a woman wearing a floor-length dress. She walked to the middle of the porch and stood stock still. Something about her made Mouse feel terribly uneasy... as if something were very, very wrong... but nothing *looked* wrong. Still, she couldn't shake the feeling.

Then two men came through the door behind her... Mouse started to panic quietly... men in the dark were never a good thing. But they simply walked up to her, one on either side, took her by the elbows and guided her off the roof, closing the door behind them.

"What *is* this place?" she finally pleaded, still feeling distressed but not understanding why. Nothing terrible had happened...

"Oh," her mother replied. "That building on the left is an orphanage; the smaller one on the right is an asylum."

"What's an asylum?" Mouse asked.

"It's a place where people who..." Polly paused just long enough for Mouse to recognize that this might be what her mother often referred to as "a delicate subject."

"Is this a delicate subject?" she asked.

Her mother sighed. "Yes," she sighed, "I guess it is. The people who live here need special help to live because they don't seem to think right. They have trouble out in the world, so this is a safe place for them."

For reasons she'd never have been able to explain, it didn't feel safe to Mouse.

She was glad to go back to Mama's and disappear into sleep. Seventy years later, just the thought of that sight would still give her the creeps.

The next day Mama wanted to take them all out to "the farm." The ride in a limousine, naturally—it was the only way she traveled—seemed endless, especially since Mouse had been told to "sit still" and so she couldn't kneel on the seat to look out the window and see everything that they were driving past which she really, really wanted to do.

Mouse was expecting to see, at Mama's farm, what she knew from the Pennsylvania hills as "a farm"—a barn and fields of things growing, maybe some cows and goats, but Mama's farm wasn't like that. After the turn into "the farm," the road seemed to go on forever and all there was to see was grass. Finally, some wooden buildings appeared ahead, to the left of the road. The chauffer pulled in and after some words from Mama, he disappeared into a house that was set back farther off the driveway.

The buildings Mouse had seen turned out to be stalls for horses and the horses, both dark brown, were in them. Annie wanted to pet them, but Mama pulled her away. They walked a little farther and came to what had appeared to be, from a distance, cages... and they were, but inside the cages were creatures the likes of which Mouse had never seen: they looked kind of like chickens but like chickens from some nightmare. They were bigger than what she knew to be chickens... not in their girth—in fact, they actually looked a little skinny to her—but in the width to which they could extend their wings. And they were wildly colorful with colors Mouse had never seen on a chicken... more like the feathers of a parrot, really.

She approached the wire cages cautiously, but before she was even an arm's length away, Mama snatched her back, speaking urgently but in Spanish. Mommy translated. "Those," she said, "are fighting cocks. You don't want to get too close; they are trained to attack. They can't get to you, of course, but they would if they could." Both of the girls backed away from the birds slowly.

Mouse, always curious, asked about the fighting and when she was told that the big birds fought other roosters like themselves and that people placed bets on the match. Innocently Mouse, who had watched the prizefighter fight on television with her father, asked how they could tell who won. Mommy translated the question for Mama, then translated it back for Mouse: "The one who's alive."

Mouse almost cried aloud.

The four of them walked a little farther so that Mama could show them the tombstone for her beloved German Shepherd, who had died not long before. Mouse had always liked graveyards, though she didn't know why she liked them; she just did. They were peaceful. She was looking forward to seeing a tombstone for a dog; she'd never seen one of those before, but what she saw was not a tombstone; it was a long, stone bench that you could sit on. The dog's name and his dates of birth and death were engraved where the back pillows might have been on a couch and the dog's remains were in the permanently sealed seat. It overlooked a large grassy area, a lovely place to sit and contemplate. It seemed lovely… but a bit odd.

She and Annie remained silent for the trip home, more than a little overwhelmed by what they'd heard that day. Mouse didn't eat much for dinner; she was already too full of too many things. She did have to be prepared for bed, though, and even the bathrooms in this strange house were strange and uncomfortable feeling. The bathroom she and Annie were to use was marble from floor to very high ceiling, and the shower was just an area in the space... no shower door or curtain, just the showerhead and a drain in the marble floor.

The sisters slept soundly that night, emotionally exhausted as they were, and awoke to preparations for church. Breakfast would come later. Mama, as a gift, had purchased extravagant white dresses for the girls, especially to wear to church. Everyone dressed and got into the limo and the driver took them from The Embassy quarter, where Mama's house was situated, to the center of Havana and the cathedral. Neither Mouse nor Annie could ever have expected what they saw when they arrived at the foot of the stairs leading to the plaza that led to the cathedral. There were more people packed more tightly in one place than Mouse had ever seen; most of them appeared to be beggars. The people nearest to the sidewalk where all the limousines were pulling up were, in fact, begging. Many of those on the stairs appeared to be wounded in some way, there were bandaged arms and legs and heads, and some were on crutches. Mama and Polly looked straight ahead as if none of this were happening around them. Mouse was mystified... and a little scared.

It felt to Mouse more as if they were entering a hospital than a church as they walked in what felt like a kind of parade of wealthy, well-dressed people that split the ragged tribe in half. It was clear that this was a conscious thing that was happening, an unspoken agreement of some sort, the poor folk making sure they did not even touch the rich folk. At the door to the church, most of the poor people stayed outside.

The cathedral was packed. Molly and Mama and the girls had to stand in the crowd at the back as all the seats were already filled. For Mouse, the service was even more boring than usual. She recognized the Latin parts but, of course, had no idea what they meant, and the rest was in Spanish, so she understood nothing. She occupied herself, though, with inspecting the churchgoers, the elaborate stained glass windows, and the detailed statuary. Finally tired of standing and having exhausted all her visual options, she dropped her chin on her chest and let her eyes close a little. As she did, she noticed that the floor beneath her feet was... not exactly a floor. It seemed to her to be some kind of thick glass, and it was dirty, no doubt from all the people who had walked on it. She thought that a glass floor was odd and began, as surreptitiously as she could, inspecting it more closely. She finally determined that something was definitely under that glass, but she couldn't quite make it out.

Just then, the time for receiving communion came. A bell had rung, and people were milling around in a semi-orderly fashion. Some headed for the railing in the front of the church as others returned. Mouse was still enraptured by the mystery beneath her feet. She held her ground as people bustled around her. Mommy and Mama left for the front, cautioning Mouse and Annie to stay put right where they were. As they left, a little more space was created and a little more light hit the mysterious glass on the floor, whereupon Mouse found herself staring into the face of a dead person. She almost screamed but managed to contain herself. After all, she'd seen dead babies in bottles in the fridge at home all the time... but this was different. This was a full-grown, dressed—albeit in rags—dried-out-looking adult human being. More than anything, she just wanted to not be standing over him, but there was no way she could move; Mommy and Mama would never find her in that mass of people. She didn't want to scare

Annie, who was occupied staring into space, so she stood her shaky ground and hoped with all her might that they'd be leaving on Monday... and they did.

Ocean City

Nana and Pop-Pop had raised their kids in Pennsylvania during the school months and, over the summers, in Ocean City, New Jersey, in their three-story house that was really a three-story stack of apartments, as each floor was a living space with three potential bedrooms, a bathroom, a fully equipped kitchen, and an undesignated space with no windows that could serve as a workroom or storage room. A small elevator had been installed so that Nana and Pop-Pop could more easily reach the third-floor level where they lived. When Mouse was there, she liked to take the elevator by herself, pretending she was an elevator operator in a big hotel.

Each floor also had a back porch that had once had a beautiful view of the beach and the ocean, but by the 1950s beach homes lined the road across the street that stretched the many blocks-long lengths of the beach. In order to make the most of the view from the third-floor porch, the railing surrounding it was only 12 inches high. Mouse generally preferred to crawl out onto the porch, terrified as she was by the thought that she might trip—or be pushed—over the edge.

A washing machine was available for general use in a small room next to a very large garage that could hold three cars or two cars and a small boat. An outdoor clothesline dryer, with a shape similar to an inverted umbrella, stood in the ever-vacant, somehow golden-yellow pebbled lot next to the house.

The washing machine may have been a little outdated, but it functioned. It had three large copper plungers that moved rhythmically up and down to agitate the clothes and a pair of rollers—called wringers—to squeeze the water out of the wet garments prior to hanging them.

Before Polly and Memo had enough income to purchase their own Ocean City home, the Mouse had been a frequent summertime visitor at her grandparent's summer home. They'd taken care of her when she was an infant and there was only room for one more person in the house because Nana and Pop-Pop slept in separate rooms because Pop-Pop snored. The room Mouse got was very tiny and did double-duty as a storage room for years of Readers Digest magazines and a beautiful old vanity that Nana used to apply her make-up.

Mouse helped with the dishes, went shopping with Nana, and spent most afternoons on the beach, walking, collecting shells—slipper shells were her favorite—and picking up discarded popsicle sticks. The popsicle sticks had a very definite function to perform, as one of the ways that Mouse would occupy herself on rainy days was to go down the street to the home of a woman she learned to call Aunt Mary. There was room to play on the floor at Aunt Mary's, which there was not at Nana and Pop-Pops. Mouse kept her "lumber truck"—a Tonka Toy with an open back for loading—at Aunt Mary's and would spend rainy afternoons sorting her popsicle sticks by shade into imagined lumber deliveries of ash and poplar and oak and so on.

Pop-Pop owned a motorboat, a wide, unspectacular-looking thing that he only occasionally got a hankering to drive. The boat was kept at a dock on the bay. Nana would always drive them there because, of course, Pop-Pop couldn't be seen driving since he was supposed to be thoroughly crippled. Once at the location, a narrow swath of land that lay between two summer weekend residences, he would use his canes to get to the boat and, from the top of the short ladder that led down to it, would toss them into the boat and climb down, willing to trust that Lady Luck would take care of providing his invisibility to the world for just that short moment, and she must have, for he was never found out.

He'd take his place, seating himself at the stern, and drop the engine down into place as Nana and Mouse settled themselves. One fine afternoon, though, Pop-Pop decided that it was time that Mouse learned to swim. He informed her of that as he gingerly stood, ensuring his secure balance with a cane, grabbed her around the waist with his free arm, and threw her into the bay. Mouse panicked and began thrashing wildly as, from the boat, her Pop-Pop began giving her instructions, the first one of which was to stop yelling.

Then he told her to "Just relax. You'll float," he said. "Just relax."

"Just relax..." where had she heard that before? It seemed so familiar. At any rate, she did relax.

"Now," he followed, shortly after she had managed to relax and had found herself to actually *be* floating... not entirely above the water, as she'd have liked to have been, but enough that she could breathe. "Paddle."

To her surprise, as she did that, her back end seemed to lift up a little. Her mind acknowledged that fact, but she still felt terribly scared. She said nothing; she just kept paddling in place. Eventually, Nana reached over the side and drew her up and into the boat. Silence ensued as Pop-Pop whisked them off for a ride farther out into the bay.

Mouse spent the rest of the day hiding-but-not-hiding in the long, low closet of Nana's bedroom. The closet was filled with old paperbacks and various boxes and cases filled with sewing paraphernalia. No one bothered her.

There were a couple more "swimming lessons" before Pop-Pop decided that it was time "for the paddler" to learn how to dive. For this event, they drove to the biggest, fanciest hotel on the beach, Flanders. Just the sight of the diving boards terrified her, but she had to admit that, at the very least, if she didn't come to the surface after the event, there were plenty of people around to collect her if that was required.

Pop-Pop had her watch the divers as they dove and gave a running commentary on "form" as they did. Finally, it was time for her to try.

There were three diving boards, each one a little higher than the one preceding it. She proceeded to the shortest board, the one closest to the surface of the water. She hadn't been—despite having watched the divers—prepared for the bounciness of the board, which seemed to spring back at her and, in fact, threw her off balance, dumping her small body, unceremoniously, off to one side and into the water. She returned to her grandparents for further tutoring.

After listening to a series of facts and instructions that she found incomprehensible, they felt that she was ready to try again. All Mouse wanted to do was to leave, but that was not within the realm of her possibilities, so she headed back to the shortest board to try again and did as they had suggested, standing in place and getting used to the bouncing for a bit. That got to feel kind of pleasant to her, so she bounced a little harder… and then a little more… and then she fell off the side.

This time, though, she returned to the board to do some more bouncing… and after bouncing a little harder and going a little higher each time, she decided that she was ready to try it… she was ready to dive and as the board lifted her, she lifted her arms above her head, just as she'd seen the real divers do, and sprang up and out, away from the board and landed flat on her belly in the water with a resounding *SMACK!* that caught pretty much everyone's attention.

The nearest of the pool lifeguards sprang from her chair and into the water to flip Mouse over and float her over to the side of the pool, where two other guards carefully lifted her from the water.

"Are you OK?" they asked, almost as one.

Mouse, slightly breathless, nodded weakly.

By this time, Nana had reached her side so that she could direct the young lady lifeguard as to where her granddaughter's mildly traumatized body might be placed. The young woman carried Mouse gently, placing her gingerly on one of the chaise lounges of choice.

Mouse was mortified, but to her great relief, neither Nana nor Pop-Pop said a thing and the next thing she knew, she was back in her small room at the beach house. There were, thankfully, no more swimming lessons.

By the time the sibling count of Mouse's family had grown to five children, though, Polly and Memo had decided that it was time they get their own home in Ocean City, and they did. It was a two-story wood structure with a partially open loft that was a ladder's climb up from the second-floor great room. The house had one bedroom downstairs, right off the kitchen, that would be Mommy and Daddy's, and two bedrooms upstairs, one of which was very large and could hold four beds.

The house was on the bay, fronting a small lagoon, so there was a dock as well. Memo bought himself a small cabin cruiser and he bought Mouse an Admirals cap and her very own rowboat, which she named Minnow. The cabin cruiser was named Conejita, after

Polly; the name was Spanish for Little Rabbit. Mouse had assumed that was because rabbits have so many babies. Only when Polly was in the last year of her life did Mouse discover, because she'd just come out and asked her mother, "When was it that Daddy started calling you rabbit, anyway?" that it hadn't been Daddy who'd given her the nickname after all.

"Oh no," she'd said gaily. "It was the boys in med school who gave me that name."

Mouse hadn't asked why.

Polly and Memo could only take a week away from work at a time, so it was decided that they would locate a reputable babysitter who could watch the kids in the shore house during the week. They would come down on weekends, and the babysitter could go home to her family. They found a young woman whom they thought would be the perfect match, a college student who was also the eldest child in a family of sixteen! Her name was Ginger; it was really Virginia, but because of a conspicuous mop of ginger-colored hair and more freckles than Mouse had ever seen on anyone, no one called her that. She was definitely a Ginger.

This meant that Mouse and Annie and Cici, who'd been born a couple of years after Annie, would all sleep in the big back room on the second floor, the room over the garage that could easily fit at least five beds in it, while Ginger would take one of the two smaller bedrooms across the hall from the bathroom.

Not long after the girls were all settled in and Polly and Memo had returned home, Ginger's friends, Janice and Joyce, showed up. They set up shop in the other smaller bedroom and soon, the six of them, three large and three small, were regularly seen, on bright sunny days, making their way from the bay to the beach, where the three older girls attracted a great deal of attention from... well... pretty much every single guy within about a nine-block radius. It was a party on the beach every day.

Mouse loved watching it all. The girls in their two-piece suits and the boys... well, the one boy, in particular, because most of them wore "swimming trunks," but one boy... the one boy... he wore a skintight, genital hugging, she-didn't-know-what-to-call-it, but she couldn't take her eyes off it.

There were parties, too, at the house at night, after "the girls" were supposed to be asleep, but the music and laughter coming from the first floor always kept Mouse awake and intrigued. She'd often creep out of the bed she'd been tucked into so that she could lie on the floor at the top of the stairs and eavesdrop on the party below. She dreamed of the time when she'd be old enough to be on her own and able to party.

Ginger had been given very specific instructions for bedtime, which involved the hateful prayer that had terrified Mouse since she'd first been forced to learn it at home: *Now I lay me down to sleep. I pray the Lord my soul to keep. If I should die before I wake, I pray the Lord, my soul to take.*

Knowing that there was every possibility that she might die—or, worse yet, be killed—in her sleep would keep her awake every night until exhaustion finally got the best of her.

But mostly, summer with Ginger and all her friends was fun. The end came all too soon and the prospect of returning to school was stultifying.

Moving, Changing Schools

Polly, a brilliant woman, was Catholic. Eventually, the beautiful house in which they lived was competing for its share of the doctors' combined finances with the requirements of the children—there were five of them by then—that was filling up the house, not to mention the cost of hired help. It was decided that the family must move to a more affordable location so that the children could continue to be properly educated. Proper education demanded proper schools and those schools were, ideally, private schools. Polly was willing to sacrifice the glamor of a fabulous house in a fabulous location in order to see that her children were educated in a manner suiting their status.

The house she'd found was only a five-minute drive from the hospital at which she was then working. The school she had her eye on for the girls—the very school where her childhood friend, Grace, had gone, a private

Catholic school catering to the upper class—was perhaps two miles from the hospital so that she could easily drop the girls off on her way to work, while the private, Quaker school for the boys was literally around the corner from the house. It was perfect.

There had been a parochial school exactly the same distance from their new home as the elite Ravenhill school, but Polly was insistent that her girls be educated among the wealthy. It was hell for Mouse. Most of the girls in her class had known each other since kindergarten. Most were white-skinned. The girls with skin color like Mouse, who took after her Cuban father, were from "the islands." Mouse would never find out what islands those were because they, like the white girls, would have nothing to do with her. In their case, though, it was because she didn't speak Spanish. Polly and Memo spoke Spanish, but only to each other. It was their way of being able to communicate privately. Doubly shunned, she and Annie walked home together every day by themselves.

One day, as they were walking up the street, about a third of the way home, a car pulled over towards the sidewalk. The driver—man—leaned over to roll down the passenger-side window as if to ask directions... but it wasn't directions that he wanted. In the outstretched hand, he held out there were two candy bars. *This again,* thought Mouse to herself as her sister began walking towards the car.

"NO!" Mouse shouted, grabbing her sister by the back of her uniform. As she did, the car took off. Mouse looked at her sister in utter disbelief. How did she not get it? She spent the next block explaining that men like that tried to catch little girls like Daddy tried to catch fish and that they wanted to take them home and keep them forever. She stopped short of explaining the worst that might happen and couldn't understand why her sister seemed so ignorant after all they'd been through.

Mouse was concerned about the state of things in general as time after time, she'd see stories in the local newspapers about young women who "claimed" that they had been abducted by some well-to-do and much-respected businessman and kept in a basement until they'd found a way to escape. The women were never believed. Never. Mouse knew that the likelihood that the women were telling the truth was pretty high. She knew because she knew that her grandfather's "friends" were just those kinds of men. She was afraid for her sister. Annie just didn't seem to be 'alert' to danger in the same way that she was.

Meanwhile, Mouse had other problems of her own at home. Mommy had put the three girls in one bedroom of the new house on the third floor. Daddy was not happy about that. He insisted that the small cedar closet across the hall be converted into a bedroom for the Mouse and so it was.

Mommy got everything set up and, on her first night in the new space, gave Mouse a small book about how girls mature and what happens to their bodies. Mouse read it numerous times. The whole "bleeding" thing concerned her. It sounded yucky. The pregnancy thing shocked her because when she had asked about how mommies got babies sometime before, her mother had said, "The daddy and mommy go into their bedroom and then he puts a seed into her, and that seed makes the baby."

Mouse had seen it clearly in her mind's eye... the bedroom was aglow in soft, orangey candlelight. They stood there, facing each other and he turned to his bureau, opening the top drawer—the really high-up one—and took out a small, clear, rectangular box—the clear, plastic kind, with the little snap-clasp. In the box were lined up what looked like five round, white pills—the seeds—and he very carefully removed one, holding it gingerly between his thumb and index finger. He turned to face Polly and as he did, she very slowly tilted her head back, just like she did when she was receiving communion, and, just as when she was receiving communion, she very delicately slid her tongue out of her mouth. With great care, he deposited the small, round seed on her tongue, and she raised her head to close her mouth and swallow the precious seed.

But no, that's not what the book said. That penis—the thing the men stuck in her vagina—the thing her father had tried to put in her so many times—the thing she grew to like sucking on instead because that made him happy and she liked it too, the softness when it was limp, the velvety feeling when it got firm, the way it filled up her little mouth—that penis had the seed and putting the penis in the vagina made the baby in the tummy... but not until you were grown up and you were grown up when that bleeding thing—which sounded AWFUL—started happening.

She couldn't stop reading the book. She read it almost every day. The book said that the bleeding started at different times for different women. She dreaded the possibility that out of nowhere—when she was at school, maybe—blood would just start gushing out of her.

Thankfully, it didn't happen that way.

It happened so slowly that she wasn't surprised by its arrival at all; she just didn't know what to do about it. She wasn't prepared. It had made its appearance shortly after she got home from school one day, not long after she'd started to experience some cramping in her tummy. She'd taken the sensation for some kind of stomachache until she'd gone to the bathroom and seen the small dark red splotches in her panties. Knowledgeable but otherwise unprepared for this particular rite of passage, she sought out Lena. Lena was their latest housekeeper.

Pop-Pop, as it turned out, did not care for having persons of color in a house that he visited perhaps twice a year. So he had determined to take on the task of choosing his daughter's 'help' if she, herself, did not take care of the matter, which she had. She'd hired someone new, she'd told Mouse on the way home from the hairdresser one day. That was all she'd said. As all the previous "help" had been persons of color, Mouse was not expecting to see an ancient white lady, let alone one who was even smaller than she was, especially because the woman's back was so badly deformed that her face presented itself lower than her shoulders. It had been a little shocking at the time.

Her mother introduced her to Lena, who looked her straight in the eye... sort of. Lena was, in the common parlance of the day, a person who was termed a "wall-eyed hunchback." Mouse had heard both those terms before but had never seen them physically embodied. She was, briefly, terrified. That ended quickly though as, still holding the ocular connection—such as it was—Lena had smiled at her and she could see, in one of her eyes anyway, a kindness that felt heartwarming. Lena was a good person. Mouse recognized that.

Unprepared in any way for the particular rite of passage she found herself in, Mouse sought out Lena and told her what was going on and that she had pain in her tummy. Lena soothed her worries, explaining that cramps were normal. She set Mouse up in a comfy chair with a heating pad and a very small glass of crème de menthe with instructions to sip it very, very slowly.

When Polly arrived home from work that evening, Lena, while standing over Mouse—sort of—told her what had occurred. Polly's immediate and oddly enthusiastic response was, "Thank God. I thought it would never come."

Mouse didn't understand her mother's response and thought that perhaps Mommy had thought that she—Mouse—was, in some way, broken, but that wasn't it at all. It turned out that she'd had some sort of 'deal' with Memo that he would "leave her alone" once she got her period.

Her mother marched her upstairs to the master bathroom, opened up the linen closet, withdrew a box of tampons from somewhere in its depths and tossed it toward her.

"You know what to do with these," she said as she turned to shut the bathroom door behind her on her way out.

The next day, Mouse returned from school to discover that her room in the closet was no longer her room. Her bed had been moved back to the "sisters" room, exactly where it had been before. It would be over now, she figured... no more visits from Daddy in the night... but she had figured wrong. What was over, though, was "the love affair" that her father had been carrying on with her. Now it was more like a term that she had heard used jokingly at school: "Wham, bam..." but not even the "Thank you, ma'am" that usually terminated the joke. The interaction would usually happen on a Friday night when he'd come home late, smelling strongly of alcohol, well after everyone was in bed.

The next morning, as a rule, and after her sisters were up and out and about, Mouse would draw herself a hot bath in the tub, climb in, and recline there, soaking for as long as she could without being bored to tears or the water turning tepid. Sometimes, after that, she'd return to the usually-vacant-by-then bedroom, pull out her Barbie dolls, and have them play-act a little drama she called "Rape by the Lake," only vaguely recalling the events in the woods years before.

Mouse was emotionally devastated. That's when she began to walk home a different way, leaving Annie to go it alone. The "new" way home had her leaving the school property by the back entrance onto a road called School House Lane on account of the number of private schools that had been established there. It was significantly less residential than the previous walk. One day it happened that one of her classmates was walking the same way and from that day forward, they walked together as far as the road where her new friend turned off to go to her house, which also happened to be a sort of connector between the old walk home and the new one. So, sometimes, Mouse would walk all the way home with her, stop off for a snack, or play with her on her Ouija board, a bizarre device that seemed like a lot of nonsense to Mouse.

Her new friend's name was Diane. She, too, coming from an Italian family, was a bit of an outcast, but her skin was far paler, and, as a result, she was not harassed or teased like Mouse was. Her father owned a business;

her mother "kept house," and Mouse had no idea what her big sister did, but she drove a Thunderbird and she was almost never there.

One day, when Diane got picked up from school for an appointment somewhere, Mouse decided not to take the turn onto the street where Diane lived. Instead, she kept walking, sure that she'd likely find a cross-street name that she recognized. By the time she'd walked way farther than she'd expected to and was beginning to get a little concerned, she did see something she recognized—the William Penn Charter School where her brothers went. She could cut right through there, she was certain, and she'd almost be home.

The trip through the grounds of the school took a little longer than she'd expected, but not because it was a longer walk than she'd expected. Mouse had discovered "practice." There were all kinds of practices going on. Outside, there was soccer and football and track; inside, though, was the best—wrestling.

Wrestling! Ahhhhh... the uniforms were FAB-U-LOUS. She could see... everything... or imagined she could. And beautiful arms and legs, as perfectly shaped as those in the pictures she'd seen of Grecian statues. But the smell was what put her over the top—it was man's smell magnified. She was in heaven, and, much as she enjoyed Diane's company on the way home, she knew that this was the way she would walk home from now on... and she did.

Eventually, someone noticed her presence there, not a teacher, not an athlete, but a student; the sort of student that in later years would probably have been designated "a slacker." He called himself Hoey, and he offered to show her around the school as well. Once he found a secluded enough stairway, he edged Mouse into a corner and began to kiss her. Pretty much programmed to respond to a male advance of that sort, she threw herself into it and before she knew it, she was on her knees watching as he unzipped his slacks... salivating for what she knew was going to follow and just as soon as he had lowered his pants, she was on him... that smell... she loved it.

It was over fast, though. He offered her his handkerchief so she could spit out the semen she'd collected, and she looked up at him, nodding a small thanks. It seemed the polite thing to do. He put himself back together again and they continued the tour, running into one of the teachers along the way. The teacher, an impressive-looking man with a hook where one of his hands should have been suggested, with the utmost politeness, that the tour was over and escorted the couple to the nearest exit.

Mouse continued on home, which was only a block away at that point. Her heart was still racing when she got there.

After not very long in their employ, Memo made Lena leave. He did not like seeing someone every day in his house, he'd said, who was "deformed." It broke Mouse's heart when he'd made Lena go away and she feared for her, hoping she'd find a place where she'd be appreciated. She felt even worse when Lena was quickly replaced with an evil husband and wife team that had been hand-picked by Pop-Pop to "keep an eye on the girls," which they would go on to do for many years, reporting back on house activity in general and later, on Mouse's every date with a boy and the hours she kept.

Mouse had been heartbroken when her mother gave her the news. Her eyes filled up with tears.

"You're too labile," her mother snapped at her. "No crying. You understand? No crying anymore. You understand?"

Mouse nodded silently. She understood. And she didn't cry again until she was in her 70s.

More Damn Dance Classes

Polly was all in on making sure that her eldest, Mouse, who looked so much like her, would establish herself as "one of the girls," one of the white girls who wanted pretty much nothing to do with her, but Mommy didn't know that. To facilitate her hopes, when Polly discovered that there were Friday night classes in ballroom dancing, she signed her very reluctant daughter up, the daughter who couldn't tell left from right, the daughter who had almost no friends in her class because she wasn't quite white... and only the white girls went to the dancing class because the brown girls, the Spanish-speaking girls, were "boarders."

The boarders lived at the school; they weren't going anywhere. Mouse had no idea where it was that they lived, but she suspected that they had bedrooms in what had once been the manor house of the estate, a manor house that now sat between two of the most uninspired brick buildings that one could imagine; they might as well have been factories. The manor house, though, had once been the school, back when Polly's friend, Grace, had gone there, but as enrollment grew, expansion was required, and available funds were not up to a task as expensive as it would have been to create a structure that looked as if it belonged there, although funds were sufficient enough to allow the construction of a large kitchen and a long, glassed-in hallway that led from the manor house to a cafeteria that was added on for the students.

The long hall had been extended to allow indoor access to a quietly elaborate small chapel that was just able to hold the school population. It was a home for a confessional as well, a confessional that demanded mandatory visitation from the student body.

Already put off by Church itself, Mouse was no fan of mandatory confession. Sins were, apparently, mandatory. "Bless me, Father, for I have sinned" could not be re-framed as, "Bless me, Father, for I have not sinned." This, in Mouse's book, was adding insult to injury. She knew who the sinners were... she was related to them! But because she had to confess something, she made things up... and that wasn't lying as far as she was concerned because she was being forced to do it. It began to seem to her as if life never got any more fair.

Now there were dance classes on top of everything else. Again. But what would she wear? The invitation had said that the mandatory attire was "semi-formal," which meant nothing to her, but Mommy knew and Daddy knew, so Daddy took Mouse shopping at the store where he liked to buy presents for Mommy which may have had more to do with the location of the store—which was right next to the hotel restaurant where he and his friends often lunched—and the staff of the store who were three flawlessly attired and exceedingly attractive young women.

Mouse felt as if she were... a doll, perhaps? Something to be dressed up and talked about and giggled over. She was certainly not a person whose opinion might matter. Daddy sat in a chair, enjoying a cocktail, as the young women presented him with options, some of which were dresses suitable for his pre-pubescent daughter who was—she so wanted to remind them—right there, for Pete's sake!

They left the shop with a brilliantly red dress that was almost strapless and consisted of more fabric than any three regular dresses. Mouse felt utterly lost in it. She was also angry that her father had paid the young woman so much attention. He was always going on, at home, in bed, about how she was his girl, but after what she'd just witnessed, she knew him for a liar.

She was not looking forward to dancing class... and it was held every other Friday... there would have to be, she imagined, more dresses; she couldn't wear the same one every week... or would she have to? How embarrassing that would be, and then... it was, after all, a dance class. The whole left/right thing was bound to come into play, but there was no way out. Mommy had paid for it. A dress had been purchased. Pictures had been taken. She was going.

The night of the class, Mommy dropped her off at the door of what looked like a brick townhouse in nearby Germantown. Cars waited in line to drop off their well-dressed boys and girls, most of whom seemed, to Mouse, to have been there before as they confidently strode up the stairs and through the door as though they lived there. She emerged from the station wagon tentatively as her mother reassured her that she'd be back to get her at 8:00.

The room in which the class was held was on the second floor. It looked like a large emptied-out auditorium. The floor was highly polished wood and the windows in the room were very tall and narrow. Chairs had been placed around the perimeter and there were already girls and boys who were seated and talking to each other, for the most part, girls talking with other girls and boys with boys. Mouse recognized some of the girls from her class, but they were all engaged in conversation, and she didn't really know them anyway, so she took a chair and waited for class to begin.

The teacher, a woman that looked to be about Mouse's grandmother's age, called the class to stand in lines: boys on one side of the room and girls on the other. She then proceeded to partner the boys with girls who were appropriately sized. Mouse was short, the shortest of the girls that were present, and she was paired, therefore, with the shortest of the boys, a young man not much taller than her with a skin tone not unlike her own. His name was Fred. Judging from his last name, he was of Italian descent.

The dance they were to learn to master that night was the cha-cha-cha. Mouse, because of her previous dance-class trauma, had been terrified at the prospect of being embarrassed in front of all her classmates, but the cha-cha-cha was a Cuban dance... she'd grown up with it... and Fred—that was her partner's name—was a natural. Before he left with his parents that night, he asked Mouse to accompany him to the Autumn Ball at the school that her brothers went to. The dance was in two weeks. She knew that she would have to ask her parents—she'd never been on a date before—she guessed this was a date... she wasn't entirely sure.

She told him that she would like to go even though she was very nervous about the whole prospect and she gave him the telephone number of the house and asked him to call her the following day because she said, she'd have to ask her parents, more specifically, she knew, she would have to ask her father. Her mother would be delighted.

As she waited for Mommy to pick her up, standing on the brick sidewalk outside the building, her mind was generating questions, the most critical one was, if they said "yes," what would she wear? She couldn't wear the very same dress she'd worn that night, but it was an expensive dress... what would she do?

She told Mommy on the way home what had happened, and Mommy was, indeed, delighted. She even offered to "run it by Daddy."

"Don't worry about a dress," she'd said. "We'll figure that out."

Two weeks later, Mouse attired in one of her mother's more demure cocktail dresses—a black dress with the thinnest of white lines creating a subtle window-pane effect and a back that was cut down to her waist—awaited the arrival of her date. Her father, angry with his wife, was pouting upstairs in his bedroom after having expressed his dismay at his daughter looking like "an adult."

When Fred knocked at the door, Polly opened it, introducing herself and waving a salutation to Fred's parents, who remained in the car in the driveway, and with that, the Mouse was on her way to her first date and the only first prize she would ever get: for dancing the cha-cha-cha with Fred.

At her door, after the dance, his parents waiting in the car, Fred attempted a quick kiss, but Mouse wasn't having it. Fred was nice, but Mouse, as she was discovering on her own, wasn't at all attracted by "nice." She had now been "seen" at the boy's school by a large audience and the walks home from school would grow ever more interesting. She didn't have to wait long.

As she approached the final few steps of her trek through the boy's school the following week, she was approached by a boy she'd not taken notice of before as he'd been a soccer player and her interests tended toward indoor sport. His hair was pitch black and a stark contrast to skin that was almost as white as milk.

He introduced himself as "Gerald." He told her that, in case she didn't know, there was a dance every Friday night in the Episcopalian church that was right around the corner from where they were standing. She'd never even noticed the church because, on her walk home, it was not in her line of sight, but she turned as he pointed and sure enough, there was a church. *It's small*, she thought. As churches went by, but then, it was an Episcopalian church... *maybe they're just smaller.*

"Starts at eight," he said.

And that Friday night, a little past 8 o'clock, she was there... having told her parents that there was "a church dance" just down the street.

"Back by ten!" they cautioned, and off she went.

She was back by nine because she was bored and new, so no one knew who she was, and the boy who'd told her about it was nowhere to be seen.

But just in case, she went back the following Friday, and she was glad she did because there he was—Gerald. He was slow dancing with a girl she'd never seen before, but a while after the dance was over, she caught his eye, and in the weeks ahead, they ended up dancing another time or two, sort of alternating with the other girl he'd been dancing with.

She became a 'regular' and soon they were dancing together more than not. The girl—Sherry—was a member of that same church, as was Gerald's family, who, as it turned out, lived right next door. Pretty soon, Gerald's house was a regular stop on her way home. She met his father—a doctor, but an administrator—his mother—from whom he'd obviously inherited his complexion and hair color—and his younger brother.

Gerald's mom was a fastidious housekeeper and a bonafide homemaker with a great figure and the most beautiful hair Mouse had ever seen. It fell to just above her shoulders and was perfectly coiffed at all times. It was what was termed "salt & pepper," black but perfectly punctuated by strands of silver. She was always dressed like someone in a television show about a "normal American family." Mouse could tell that Gerald's mom was not overly thrilled with her, but she didn't know why.

She did know that mothers sometimes "didn't approve" of certain boys. Her friend, Patsy, whom she sometimes saw on weekends, had a boyfriend that her mother didn't like. Patsy had matured early and in the style of Marilyn Monroe. The young man was definitely a few years older than most of their classmates, out of school and working at his father's gas station, which was, apparently, another problem. His family, even though they lived in a very nice house in a very nice neighborhood, was "working class." Girls that went to the school that Grace Kelly went to didn't date boys who worked at gas stations. Mouse didn't understand why that would be, and since she didn't work at a gas station, she couldn't imagine what it might be that was wrong with her. It had to be something. There must be something that was wrong with her, too, but she had no idea what that was.

Maybe she'd seen them kissing. Maybe that was it. Maybe she was worried about the sex. Well, she couldn't concern herself with that.

Expanding Horizons

By the time Mouse was in her freshman year at the new school, she had been bored senseless. She'd been perusing encyclopedias since she was about five years old, and she found so-called 'learning' tedious. She didn't like memorizing things and didn't see the point in it when you could just look it up. Between the uniforms and all the rules and enforced confession-going, she'd had it with the academy. She'd have stayed home 'sick' every day if she could have, but that's especially difficult to pull off when your parents are doctors.

It took her a while to devise a plan to have at least some relief from her enforced schooling experience. The first thing she had to do was to master her father's signature. There was no way she could ever duplicate her mother's signature, which looked like something out of The Palmer Method of Handwriting. Her father's, though, looked like scribble, predictable scribble, but scribble all the same. It didn't take long for her to master his style and once she did, her life changed for the better.

She knew that she couldn't get away with it too often or she'd be caught, but she could probably manage it once in a while, maybe every three weeks or so... thus her mini-sabbaticals began. She began by simply going to the Philadelphia Library instead of going to school. The local branch was actually perilously close to the school, but she figured she'd chance it. After all, once she was on the sidewalk, and it was after 3:00, she might just be walking home that way. Same for heading in, as long as she kept her eyes open and was alert, she felt she'd be fine... and she was. After all, the library opened later than school opened.

She'd find herself an empty table, which was easy as most of the tables *were* empty, then scout the shelves looking for interesting things to read and settle in for the day. With a notebook and pen beside her on the table, she would make occasional notes to make it appear that she was researching. Never once did the librarians question her presence there in the middle of the school week. She felt grateful for that kindness.

After a few months of skipping out locally, Mouse decided that it was time to broaden her horizons. She remembered well the unwanted train ride to Pottsville years before; the process seemed easily doable, so she determined to spend her next day off in New York City. There were two places in particular that interested her: The New York Library and Greenwich Village, which she'd both read about and heard a lot about, so three weeks later, instead of walking in the direction of the school, she found herself in the train to Philadelphia Station to purchase a ticket to NYC!

The Library—the steps alone—overwhelmed her... but it was fabulous, an experience more like going to the art museum than it was like going to the library at home, but it was Greenwich Village that won her heart... the bookstores were like heaven... soooo many kinds of fascinating and funny books and cards. One book, called The Curious Sofa, she would pass on to her daughter one day. She almost lost track of time and felt some anxiety about making it back in time for the train home, but she'd paid strict attention to her path there and didn't miss a turn on the way back, arriving in East Falls not much later than she would generally arrive at home, her two small book purchases tucked safely away in her book bag. She knew that she couldn't chance an excursion like that too often and only went once more as local boys began to be of rising interest.

This was the year that a group of mothers had decided that their daughters were old enough for a special treat and rented out a small second-floor apartment in Ocean City, New Jersey, dropping about eight of them off to spend an early summer weekend on their own. They had brought some supplies along for dinner, spent all day Saturday on the beach, heated up their frozen dinners, and sat down to play cards.

When the soda and chips ran low, Mouse was tagged to go down the block to the small convenience store and re-stock. They pooled their funds and off she went. About halfway to the store, a burly young man came running out of a house right toward her. She stepped back to get out of his way and was too slow to recognize that it was her that he was aiming for. He lowered his upper body, like a football player on a run to tackle, and, in fact, tackled her, swooping her off her feet and throwing her over his shoulder.

"Put me down," she screamed again and again. "Put me down."

There were a few people coming and going in and out of the store, so she cried out, "Help!" But no one paid her any attention, most likely thinking that what was going on was all in fun. She was terrified.

The boy made a sharp right turn, heading up a path that led to the door of a house where there was clearly a party going on. Mouse did not let up as he toted her in and through the writhing mass of dancing male and female bodies. She was kicking and screaming as he threw open a door, walked in, and slammed the door behind them, throwing her forcefully onto the bed. She landed on her back, facing up, and gasped, out of breath from the jolt, just as he pulled a very large knife out from somewhere.

"Shut up," he commanded.

She did.

Tossing the knife to the floor, he pinned her to the bed and began an attempt to pull her clothes off but knowing the knife was out of reach and smelling the alcohol on his breath, she fought him. He held her captive there, pinned to the bed beneath his body, through the night, both of them alternately falling asleep and fighting. Ultimately, he grew so tired that he simply rolled off her in his sleep, and, moving as furtively as she could, inch by inch, she made it out from under him, rolled slowly to the floor, using her arms to ensure that she'd fall quietly, and then took off as fast as she could. The outer room was littered with passed-out partygoers, none of whom seemed to notice as she moved stealthily through them to the door.

Her classmates were all asleep when she got back to the small apartment, with the radio still on, so she found an open mattress and crashed. She fell asleep to the news of one of the Kennedy babies dying. No one heard a thing and, come morning, no one even asked where she'd been. She'd never felt so alone.

Exploring Relationship

Because Gerald's mom was always home and hers wasn't, Mouse began sneaking Gerald into the 'den' that her father had set up in the basement. She couldn't do it during the week when Pop-Pop's spies were around, but since, on the weekends, they usually returned to Tamaqua, where their kids and grandkids lived, and her parents went to the shore house with the younger kids, leaving her "in charge of the house," she made the most of her freedom.

The basement was a hodge-podge of stored items, one of which was the piano which Mouse was still being forced to "practice" on whenever her mother could catch her. She still hated it. The piano had been an integral part of "the bar" in their previous house, where it had seen a lot of use during the many parties that were held there. That had been a much more pleasant place, at least, for Mouse to be confined with a gigantic instrument she had no interest in whatsoever. Having to fulfill her musical duties in what felt like an underground cave held far less appeal. The den, however, was a real plus. Daddy had a microscope and slides and other work-related items on an oak table with a matching chair and, in the far corner, was an overstuffed, faux leather recliner where Mouse spent time with him and where she spent time with Gerald when he and Mommy were elsewhere. Her brothers and sisters knew very well where she was, although not necessarily what she was doing, because most of them were too young to know what could possibly be going on.

Then some issues came up. The first thing that came up was that she discovered that Gerald was still seeing Sherry. It happened one afternoon when she had decided to take a different route home than she usually did and spotted them both together, walking up the stairs toward the townhouse where she lived. Mouse was furious; he'd lied to her.

Then came the "debutante ball" that he had, apparently, been committed to by his mother some months before he'd met Mouse. He couldn't get out of it because his mother said he couldn't get out of it. Mouse was more unhappy than furious with that, but she understood it. This was "society," and she was not a part of that, nor did she want to be... too many damn rules.

But the most serious challenge of all was when she discovered—because he told her about it—that he was part of a group of young men who spent numerous Sunday afternoons having sex with the wife of the couple who were the "leaders" of the youth group at the church he attended.

Mouse had met the woman—and her husband—at one of the Friday night dances. She was livid. How could he? How could *she*? And then he told her that it was all okay because her husband was right there, and it was all about teaching the boys at church how to make love to a woman. They always had a group bar-b-que after.

How on earth, Mouse wondered, *could bar-b-que make anything about that any better?*

She couldn't get it all out of her head. It simply would not go away. It kept her up that night and the next day, she determined to do something about it. She knew their names; she knew where they lived; she knew how to use directory assistance. She called the couple the following night. The wife answered the phone and Mouse lit into her.

The woman talked down to Mouse, telling her that when she was older, she'd understand. Mouse gave up and slammed down the phone. She recognized that there was nothing she could ever say that would make even a dent in the woman's righteous claims of being an advocate for youth sexuality. Gerald was horrified when she told him what she'd done, mostly because he knew that they knew that he'd been the one to let the cat out of the bag.

Mouse stopped going to the Friday night dances on general principles. Gerald stopped out of embarrassment, but he also stopped attending the Sunday afternoon soirees. Mouse was satisfied… for the moment. But when summer came and Gerald took a summer job as a scrub at the local hospital, Mouse surprised him at lunch one day, discovering him walking hand-in-hand down the hall with a young female companion.

Mouse and Gerald continued to date, but she never took it seriously again, though she wasn't seeing anyone else. They'd graduate high school soon and he'd be going miles away. They continued to have sex, but she'd ceased to find it titillating. She felt as if she were in a kind of limbo, unused to not wanting sex... and then came a surprise: her parents were moving again. Her boyfriend, though, was moving darn near all the way up the east coast. He was still trying to hold onto their relationship... but why? And she'd have to leave behind a good friend that she'd just gotten to know over the last year or so and really liked, named Suzanne.

Her friend, who'd been seeing the guy from the gas station, had gotten pregnant by him. The nuns at school had pulled Mouse out of class one day to interrogate her. It seemed to Mouse as though they were blaming her for her friend's pregnancy which was vastly confusing to Mouse.

Her mother tried to assuage her about the move by offering to drive her back to school every day since it was on her way to work. But whyever, would she want to go back there? The school was horrible as far as she was concerned. Who blames a girl's best friend for her friend's pregnancy? Those nuns and all that God stuff—she didn't like being forced to say prayers and go to confession once a week. She had her own ideas about the unseen world and "God" because if there were such a thing as an all-powerful God, how did he let so many people get away with so many horrible things? And what had she and Annie ever done to deserve what had happened to them... and the other little ones? Mouse wanted to get away from everything Catholic, but she hated to leave her friends behind, especially her boyfriend with his wandering eye, but since he'd be off to college anyway... there was little point in fussing.

Nether Providence

Pop-Pop's in-house spies—Fred and Ethel, as Mouse liked to call them (privately, of course)—would move with them. Fred went to "the new house," which was a bit over an hour away, every day for a couple of weeks to clean and make it ready for the furniture to be moved in.

About an hour after the movers had emptied out the current house, Polly loaded up the station wagon with the kids and off they all went to a place called Wallingford, which was outside of Philadelphia, to move into their new home.

They turned a corner off the big road they'd been on onto a small two-lane road with houses lined up on either side of the road. They weren't exactly identical, but neither were they as different from one another as the houses in Philadelphia had been, where every house on the block was distinctly different from its neighbor unless it was a "twin" and literally attached to its neighbor.

They turned right at the next corner, then turned into the second driveway on the left, where sat the most adorable house Mouse had ever seen. It looked like something out of a storybook. It was built of stone, only one story high, and with an actual, tiny turret on one corner. What she took for the garage door, though, seemed awfully big. She was a little confused. The house was way too tiny for their family, and the house on the left side of the driveway—which looked very much like a regular house—had its front door facing the street they'd just been on, and they'd gone right past its driveway.

What she saw straight ahead confused her still more. It was built of stone, just like the like smaller storybook-looking house, but it was long and low and entirely windowed. *Only one story with a flat top... a porch, maybe,* she thought, *but with no fencing around it?* A second story was clearly visible up there with a door that led out onto the flat area.

As her mother drove closer, she saw... well... what looked a lot like a turret. It was at the corner of a narrow open porch—more of a walkway, really—that was going around the outside of the house. As they rounded the corner, she saw a small curving set of stairs in a turret that led to the walkway as it continued around all the way to the front door. She could see the stone that covered the wall of the house itself there, punctuated by a single window, then, a bit farther down, the porch, an entire bank of windows. That area was entirely enclosed by the glass along with the front door.

The driveway led to what she would learn was called a porte cocher which was French for the place where you park the coach or, in this case, the station wagon. From there, one could go left or right to walk up two low-rise steps that led to a kind of landing area which was up relatively high as it had been originally intended to allow people to traverse, via a small, wooden 'bridge' that would be drawn out from the inside of a coach, to bridge the gap between the coach and the landing. Then it was up a couple of steps and through the glass doors of the enclosure that was protecting the actual front door, which was a beautiful, polished wood with clear leaded glass. Beside the door, on the right, was a bank of leaded glass windows, and a bit past them, a regular-looking door that led a person out of the glass enclosure and back to the rest of the open, red-tiled walkway that encircled that portion of the house, a large room that may once have served as a library.

The "house" sat on the top of a hill, overlooking four or five ordinary-looking homes at the bottom of the hill.

Home? This was home? Mouse was speechless and so were her siblings. This was no house; it was a castle and, as she would discover, it actually was a castle. It had been brought over, piece by piece—with the exception of the protective glass enclosure outside—from Europe as a wedding gift for a very privileged young man from an exceedingly wealthy family. It had been vacant for many years as no one wanted to foot the kind of heating bills that were involved, and most families just didn't have enough people to need a house that big.

The three oldest girls would each have their own rooms, on the third floor, at the front of the house. The horrible uncle, who'd still maintained a room at the

Midvale Avenue house but was rarely there (thank heaven), had gone back to Cuba to join Fidel Castro's uprising. Mouse was particularly grateful for that as she loved to keep a mouse as a pet and he loved to kill them if he got the chance, saying that vermin don't belong in a house, so she hadn't had a pet in quite a while.

Fred and Ethel had their own room at the far end of the second-floor hall, above the kitchen, and the boys were split up between the other two 'minor' second-floor bedrooms on the kitchen side of the house. Polly and Memo had the whole front of the house on the second floor to themselves. The suite even had a sliding door that could effectively cut it off from the rest of the second floor. A small hallway ran between his bedroom and hers and also opened into the master bathroom, which had the strangest shower in it that anyone had ever seen. It was made from a series of copper pipes curved into partial circles that attached to two vertical pipes in the back—the sources of hot and cold water. The base of the shower was like a bowl with very low sides; it was made of marble. A shower curtain hung around it to contain the shower itself.

The tub and sink were marble as well. Lead-paned windows spanned the entire front of the room, overlooking the top of the porte cocher and the grassy hill that sloped down towards the regular houses and the road.

None of the other bathrooms in the house were that fancy, but the house itself certainly was. The furniture that they'd brought with them looked out of place in the castle, but Memo went to work on setting that right by ordering a billiard table to go in the large entertainment room at the rear of the first floor, just beyond the entrance hall. This was as close as he'd ever been, in the states, to the kind of luxury he'd grown up with.

The floor of the soon-to-be billiard room was tiled and the walls, like those in the entrance hall, were paneled with dark wood. A very large overhead tiffany-style light hung over an old pool table in the front of the room while another, smaller version of the lamp hung over a spot that had clearly been designed for a card table. To the left of that area was a small alcove with a very large fireplace in it. On either side of the fireplace were high, narrow wood-paneled alcove-like areas where wood for the fireplace could be stacked. But what

Mouse thought was the most fun about the room was the hidden door behind the bar area. It looked like a part of the dark wood-paneled wall. Unless you knew right where to push, it *was* a part of the wall. It served as a quick way to get to the kitchen by way of a very small laundry room that just about fit the washer and dryer.

The kitchen, too, was a very large room with a strange floor that looked as if it had been made of baked clay painted deep red. In places where the surface had been damaged, you could see the original beige-y color of whatever the clay-like substance was. The deep red paint would color the wash water a dull brick-like color every time the floor was mopped, yet the color of the floor never seemed to fade.

That floor extended, at the very back, into a small pantry that looked as if it had once served as an icehouse room. The room was not heated, and one wall was composed entirely of small safe-box-sized wood-fronted, metal-lined cabinets that had what seemed to be drip trays on their bottoms. It looked as if they'd most likely been used for cold storage, but they'd end up being used simply for overflow.

Sharing the same flooring and serving as a connector between the kitchen and the dining room was a room Polly called "the butler's pantry." It was a very narrow, long space with one window at the end. It had two side-by-side, very old-fashioned-looking copper sinks with tall faucets that rose about twelve inches above the sink and delicately curved over it from above.

Just above the sinks—and the place where the dishwasher would go—was a very long two-shelf, glass-fronted cabinet that extended the whole length of the structure below. This was, apparently, for fancy glassware. While some glassware found its way there, it would become a spot where people put things that didn't seem to have anyplace else to go.

The kitchen itself had large windows on the driveway side—the driveway went clear around the house—and it had a door that opened onto a small, useful but unattractive, raised concrete porch. It was the sort of place where things might be delivered or contractors might come and go.

The house looked nothing like Memo's home in Cuba, but it must have spoken to him of the kind of wealth he'd come from, grown up with... sort of. As he'd been sent away to boarding school in America from first grade on, he'd only ever spent summers in Havana, but that seemed to have been enough to instill in him the kind of taste that he had for luxury... and for getting what he wanted because, as the only son, he had been put on a pedestal.

Memo's father, also a doctor, died that year, probably content, from where he stood, that his son was doing OK.

The bedrooms, of which there were many, were assigned by Polly. Each of the oldest girls had her own room. The boys, as before, bunked together, although not literally in bunk beds as they had been in the previous house. Fred and Ethel's very big room over the kitchen and at the end of the second-floor hallway was a perfect spot for keeping an eye on the boys on weekends when Polly and Memo went to the shore house. They'd have a good overview of what was going on kid-wise.

The horrible uncle had not moved with them. He had returned to Cuba to fight for the Revolution. That, alone, made life just a little more bearable for Mouse.

The elementary school was just down the street, and the High School was within easy walking distance. There was a bus that picked up the high school students and stopped right at the crossroad just down the street, but Mouse had tried it once and she didn't like anything about it. The girls had ignored her; the boys were way too friendly; the bus driver was curt, and everything smelled funny. Walking was better for her. Annie preferred the bus and Fred dropped all the younger ones off at the elementary school, though they walked home.

Polly decided that, in the long run, it would be more economical if she got a smaller, more convenient car for driving all the way into town, which she would do as soon as Mouse got her driver's license. That way, Mouse could take her younger brothers and sisters to doctors' appointments or go food shopping if needed and drive herself and Annie to school if it was raining.

The lessons started the day after Mouse's 16th birthday. It was only then that her father, who was teaching her how to drive, as well as still occasionally creeping into her bedroom at night when he wasn't supposed to be, learned the hard way that his eldest child and part-time reluctant lover had a serious case of left/right discrimination. Happily, it only cost him a fender. He hired a teacher, nevertheless.

After the initial left/right incident, the driving went well... her driving, that is. For whatever unfortunate reason, though, for that first year, she seemed to have become, to some degree, a kind of accident magnet. She was in three accidents before the school year would end, none of which had been her fault.

Accident #1: a head-on collision while going around a tight blind curve. She had no way to see that the young man out driving his father's Jaguar XKE on the sly had determined to take the curve so tightly as to be in her lane. She, in a sturdy station wagon, was just fine, as was the boy, but the car was a little the worse for wear, while the front end of the Jag somewhat resembled an accordion.

Accident #2: T-boned by a trolley car. This was an accident that should never have happened. It took place where there was a trolley car track that crossed a main road. There was a level crossing on the road at which point, on both sides of the track, a so-called 'gate' was supposed to come down if and when the trolley was to cross the road.

The gate was up, and traffic was moving on the opposite side of the road. Mouse drove her mother's little VW bug across the track and was hit, albeit very slowly, on the passenger's side, by an oncoming trolley.

Accident #3: rear-ended on a hill in a snowstorm. While out on an errand for her mother, in her mother's VW, with one of her two younger sisters in the back seat, it began to snow. It was light snow, just the sort that makes it pretty much impossible to brake quickly in heavier cars. On a modest incline, in the center of town, with her little sister in the back seat for safety's sake, Mouse gently applied her brakes as she approached a slowdown in traffic. No problem.

Then, WHAM! A woman in a full-sized American car slammed into the rear end of the VW so vigorously that her little sister ended up with her nose on the dashboard, unhurt but far from calm.

Mouse had become a dependable mode of transportation for her mother and Polly wasn't about to lose that. Annie, because of her accident, would never have the kind of brain power that it took to drive, and the next possible driver was a few years away. The meeting with the insurance adjuster took place at the back table in the billiard room. It consisted of the adjuster, both Memo and Polly, and Mouse. Polly was outraged that this was even an issue; after all, not one of the incidents had been Mouse's fault.

The adjuster was willing to admit that the girl was not at fault, but she was, he said, what the insurance company referred to as "a high-risk individual," and so, if they wanted her to be insured, it would have to be at a new rate. And so, it was and that was that.

New School, New Friends

Mouse was a pretty girl. She was also a mixed-race girl. She was also, as anyone could see, a product of the upper middle class. Not everyone in the public high school was upper middle class, but they were all, as far as Mouse could see, white. She and Annie seemed to be the only olive-skinned people there.

Because she could, she signed up to be an art major, which meant that she had art class every... single... day. She was thrilled! She and her mother were still not seeing eye-to-eye on her college-bound "direction," but she still loved both drawing and painting and to be able to have that opportunity every day was a lot like having recess every day like little kids had. Plus, as it turned out, a significant number of the schools' male athletes took art as they were required to add an elective class to their roster and art class was a lot less demanding than music or academics.

Mouse hadn't been in school with boys since she'd been very young... she knew a lot more about them by now and she could tell from the way that they looked at her that they knew something about girls. Art class felt very... flirty... because it was a lot less structured than the academic classes and a modicum of chatter was tolerated.

There was one person in the class, though, that made her wonder. The person was dressed kind of like a Philadelphia bus driver and had longish, dirty-looking brown hair that was pulled back into a ponytail. The overall effect was of a heavy-set older man, but under the heavy tan shirt and jacket, it looked as if there might be breasts. When the roll was taken, Mouse learned that this person was named Susan and Susan could draw like Rembrandt. Susan was an amazing artist and, besides Mouse, possibly the only person in the class who was actually interested in art and not just there to pass the time. Susan had her eye on going to the very same college that Mouse's mother wanted her to attend.

Mouse wanted to go to the University of Pennsylvania and major in journalism. She loved to write and had already been published in a national magazine for girls called Ingenue. Her poetry had received a full two-page spread, complete with her picture, but it was something that she could never show her mother. She would have been furious. Polly wanted her daughter to focus on one thing and one thing only: art. Why she did would forever remain a mystery!

Art class, as a major, threw Susan and Mouse together every day and since the other girls in the class pretty openly viewed Mouse as competition, Mouse and Susan developed a friendship. While Mouse dated several different guys at the school and even made friends with a few, Susan would be her only female friend and the following year, they would end up as fellow commuters on the train to Philadelphia.

Mouse's father, contrary to instructions from her mother, was still showing up in her bedroom from time to time at night, and she knew that he still favored her.

That ended, however, the evening of the morning that she'd arisen only to walk about ten steps and had then fainted dead away. She awoke sometime later in a puddle of lumpy blood that had pooled around her hips.

The night before, she had informed her mother that her period hadn't come. It was, by then, two weeks later than it should have been. Her mother had given her one pill that she was to take right then while she watched. She'd swallowed the pill, headed off to bed and fell asleep directly. The next thing she knew, it was morning and the next thing she knew after that was that she couldn't even get up off the floor where she lay, and there it was that she fell back asleep. Waking sometime later, feeling stronger, she realized that it was too late to go to school and obviously, no one had noticed her not showing up to get breakfast or make lunch, so she headed to the bathroom to clean herself up—and then clean the floor—and she went back to bed.

Mouse reported the incident to her mother when she arrived home that evening. Her mother acknowledged it with a curt, "We're going to the drugstore after dinner," which they did. Polly went straight to the pharmacy as Mouse perused the make-up aisle. Back in the car, before departing for home, her mother tossed her purchase—still in the bag—at her and began to explain birth control pills to her as she drove home.

"You go back when you need more and don't miss a day, or they won't work."

Well, thought Mouse to herself, *these will come in handy.*

Prom

Mouse may have had only one girlfriend in high school, but she had a couple of male friends with whom she very much enjoyed talking about life and the world. They'd spend hours in philosophical conversations without so much as a hint of anybody coming on to anybody. She loved it, but when it came toward the end of the year and prom loomed in the future, it was the captain of the football team—also a member of her art class—who asked her. She was still in touch with her high school boyfriend up at Dartmouth and had taken the bus up to visit a few times, but that hadn't held her back from either dating or having sex with other boys… but prom was special and she knew that his bringing her to the prom was a big deal.

Once more, come the big night, she found herself in one of her mother's dresses again, a floor-length emerald green sheath that was only barely discernable beneath waves of emerald green chiffon. It was lovely, if impractical, for dancing which was what prom was all about, but that conversation was not going to happen. She'd have to make do because she loved dancing and there was no way she would sit by and watch... she couldn't have, really. Dancing was still an irrepressible passion.

When her date came to pick her up, her father was with her. "I've never even met the boy," was his excuse. He'd never met any of her dates before! Mouse's face displayed her annoyance, to which he'd responded. "Don't worry. You can date anyone you want, as long as it's not a nigger or a Jew... these public schools... you just don't know."

Mouse suppressed a gasp, horrified to imagine that her father was prejudiced. *How could that be?* she wondered. *And why?* Prejudice of any sort infuriated her. She was silently relieved that he hadn't known that she'd had a crush on a beautiful black boy back at the house in Philly and had dated a Jewish boy for quite some time. She'd actually gone so far as to try to openly flirt with the black boy, but he'd turned away from her so obviously every time that she was mystified, guessing—incorrectly, she'd realize decades later—that it was because she was dating one of his classmates. At that age, she'd still not caught on that racial prejudice was a very real thing in the world around her. At that moment, after her father's comment, she got it, and her appreciation of her own ignorance overtook her father's dreadful remark.

When Tim came to the door, she let him in as her father slowly walked up behind her, assessing the young man, but something outside caught his eye. He looked at her date directly in the face. "Your car?" he asked.

Tim nodded.

Mouse went into what would be a brief state of "Now what?"

"Can I have a look?" asked her father in a tone so respectful that she was stunned.

Suddenly this was all about the car. The two of them went outside, where Tim's shiny Corvette sat under the porte-cochère.

Many questions were asked and answered.

"Could I get in?" her father asked in a tone she had never before heard.

What the hell, thought Mouse to herself, *is going on here?*

After a significant amount of male bonding had occurred, Memo turned back towards the house, leaning over to give his daughter a kiss on the way by and taking advantage of the moment to whisper, "I like this boy."

Mouse breathed a sigh of relief as Tim opened the passenger door to allow her entrance.

Prom was dull. Pictures were taken. People sat with the people they always sat with, and Mouse felt as if she were more or less just along for the ride. The music was okay but not particularly inspiring and Tim, apparently, wasn't much of a dancer, so the dress wasn't much of an issue.

The dress wasn't much of an issue, that is, until they got to the After-Prom, which was going on—and apparently had been going on—for quite some time. Mouse was in a state of wonder as Tim headed off to somewhere she'd never even known existed, to a one-story house in the woods that resembled something one might have seen in a place called "shanty town," but this was no shanty-town, newish cars were parked all around with some older cars mixed in here and there. Cars were everywhere, all over the surrounding property, under the trees, and, as Tim opened his door, she could hear music, darn good dance music... music she could go nuts too. She didn't even ask any questions when he came round to open her door. She just hiked the dress up as far as she could and high-tailed towards the open door, clutching his arm for balance.

The music was loud and potent. Her whole body was in motion before she was even conscious of it, her dress hiked up as far as she could get it. Tim was not much of a dancer, but that didn't bother Mouse even a little; as long as *she* could dance, all was right with the world.

So wrapped up in her own little world was she that she had at first failed to notice that most of the folks in the room were dark-skinned. *Where did they come from?* she wondered. There were no so-called "colored" kids in school... but these kids were every shade of brown you could imagine. This was too much fun to be wasting time on thought, she finally figured, letting loose.

It would take her about fifty years to figure out that they must have been kids from the nearby high school that was "in town" and that it was likely that the football players had gotten this thing together.

The "After Party" went on till well after 2 AM when everyone headed out and Mouse found herself at a "Breakfast Party" that was being held in some sort of auditorium-like place. She had no idea where she was, but she was definitely hungry.

Various cliques of people formed and, of course, all the athletes were in the same place. Mouse was very much focused on food and the next thing she knew, she was being shuffled back to Tim's car and they were headed for Ocean City, New Jersey.

Mouse and Tim arrived at a motel in Ocean City very early in the morning, utterly exhausted. Tim booked a room while Mouse waited in the car; then they both made their way up the outdoor staircase to the second-floor room, both of them still dressed for prom.

They slept all morning and into the afternoon when they were awakened by what could only be called 'a racket.' Horns were honking; other horns—actual horns—were being used badly, and there was a lot of raucous-sounding conversation. They made their way to the window only to see numerous grown men wearing dress shirts and bathing suits driving what looked like motorized children's cars and tricycles. There were dozens of them, and they partied all day. It made no difference to Mouse and Tim; they hadn't been planning on sunning by the pool. Neither of them even had a bathing suit, though the motel had provided fluffy white terry-cloth bathrobes and Tim had thoughtfully brought along a change of clothes for both of them, much to her surprise.

Not much to her surprise, though, they spent most of the day in bed, though he'd run out at one point to pick up a steak since the room was equipped with a micro-mini kitchen that sported a toaster oven. He'd figured that Mouse would cook it for him. They had steak once a year at Mouse's house on New Year's Day because every year, a friend of her father's would make him a gift of steaks for everyone, but Mouse wasn't the cook. Still, she'd figured, how difficult could it be?

Sometime after she'd set the steak in the toaster oven to grill, she made an attempt, with what silverware was available, to turn the steak over, but it didn't go well. She'd mistakenly tilted the small, flat pan that fits in the oven allowing the accumulated fat to spill onto the electric element at the bottom of the device and the next thing she knew, there were flames shooting out of the toaster oven toward the ceiling.

Tim was napping and her shrieking did not cause even the slightest movement in his prone body, so she did the only thing she could think to do, opened the door to the room, and ran out in her underwear carrying, with potholders, the flaming steak on the small tray. She set it down on the porch and returned with the pitcher of ice water, thinking to quell the fire, which it did... a little bit... but the fat flew, burning her legs a bit. She was too panicked to even feel it at the time and too embarrassed as well because, below her, she was being stared at by all the conventioneers, two of which, equipped with what seemed to be power-charged water sprayers, ran up the stairs to assist her in her task. Success! Sort of!

The fire was put out. The Lulus—as she learned the group was called—were vastly amused and delighted to be of service, but the manager of the hotel was not and they were asked to pay for the damages and leave, which they did.

She arrived home before her parents, who had headed off the shore with some of the kids and were not yet home.

The Long-Distance Relationship

Mouse was in Pennsylvania; Jerold was in New Hampshire and that was how it was going to be for four years. Mouse had completed her senior year in high school as he was wrapping up his freshman year in college. Jerold was Med-School bound eventually and there was not yet any idea where that might take him, but both of them were somewhat committed to their relationship. She'd caught him holding hands with another girl, but he'd sworn there was nothing more than that. He'd never caught her doing anything, but she figured that what he didn't 'know... he didn't need to know, so the relationship went on, with her taking a bus to New England every once in a while and him visiting her when he returned to the Philadelphia area... but then, his parents moved... to Detroit.

His father had received a job offer that promised both more money and more power. It was irresistible. Now Jerold could not kill two birds with one stone, so, mostly, Mouse had been traveling—by bus—to see him at school when she could. Then, come summer, he suggested that she travel to Detroit and join him there for a week or so. Mouse was iffy on the point; she'd rather have had him come stay with her for a week, if only because there were pretty much no rules at her house, and she knew that his parents—especially his mother—were all about propriety and what-not. Ugh!

But he was insistent that they go, so she went. He met her at the airport, and they drove into the posh suburban area where the new home was. She'd never been at the mercy, as it were, of his mother before and her disapproval was palpable. Mouse, having endured so much abuse as a child, was alert to the smallest changes in someone's mood or attitude. She was, essentially, always ready to run. Jerold's mother was wound as tight as Mouse was loose and when Mouse discovered that she had been scheduled, on the following day, to go shopping with this woman, she was furious, but she couldn't express that, not there, not within the confines of that house. She was going shopping with her mother-in-law-to-be and that was that. Jerold would be accompanying his father to the office to see what that was like. Mouse wasn't sure who'd gotten the better deal... if there was one.

Shopping turned out to be every bit as demanding an event as she had imagined, looking at china patterns, looking at the crystal, looking at silverware. Why? Why? She could not recall a more boring time.

It had never occurred to her that she was being observed—that her taste was being assessed. This wasn't so much "shopping" as it was an exploration. She did not know that, however, and was vastly uncomfortable.

The next day, however, was a day she'd actually looked forward to as it involved "a boat ride." The first surprise was "the boat," which was not so much "a boat" as a yacht, a really, really big yacht. She'd been imagining a Chris Craft motorboat or something equally fun. The yacht, as far as she was concerned, was not fun; it was just big. It was like a living room on the water. So what? She and Jerold sat on the bow for the trip out to what looked like, from a distance, and, indeed, turned out to be a very small island. There were docks all around at which were parked boats of equal and even larger size to the one they were on.

Jerold explained to her that this was a private island with a restaurant on it. Only boats 50 feet and longer could dock there, he'd said.

Big money. Mouse was a little creeped out but didn't know why... and wouldn't for almost another forty years.

Once inside, she was startled to find herself in a room with one very long table that ran the entire length of a very narrow room. She was even more creeped out when the 'menu' was offered and even more so when the food was served. The menu involved offered guests one choice: "How do you like your steak served?"

A few large bowls of salad were distributed across the length of the table so that diners could occupy themselves while they waited for their plate-sized steaks to arrive. This was an excess that Mouse had never been exposed to. It appalled her to the point of making her lose her appetite entirely. The fact that most of the steaks had been ordered "bloody" added to her discomfort. She could hardly wait to leave, but this would be no quick meal.

When it finally came time to go, the sun was lowering in the sky and the view from the bow looked like inspiration for a painting. Relieved to be out of the atmosphere of gluttony, Mouse relaxed a little, cradled in Jerold's arms. Rocked by the gentle wavelets in the bay, she felt as if she might fall asleep then Jerold spoke up. Her ear was just about where his mouth was, and he spoke softly… so softly that the subtle clapping of the small waves drowned out his voice.

She turned, pulling away slightly so that she could face him, and asked him what it was that he had just said.

"Will you marry me?" he responded.

Mouse almost froze in place. Marry? She wasn't even in her twenties yet. Marry?

"No!" she said, surprise coloring her refusal. "No, Jerold," she repeated more softly. "I'm not ready for that."

She felt his body droop beneath her. She was sorry to have had to hurt him; she knew she had.

No words were exchanged until they arrived back at his parent's house when he bid her goodnight. *So, that's what that whole shopping trip with his mother had been about,* she thought to herself. She didn't know what to think, what to do, or how to act. She was apparently letting the whole family down… but she was surprised by that because she knew darn well that they just weren't that crazy about her… but, of course, they did love their son, something she was not wise enough to consider at the time. His disappointment would be theirs as well. Mouse didn't know about that kind of parental love. All she wanted was to go home.

College

Per her mother's dictate—her mother who had accompanied her and sat in on her interview—Mouse attended the college of her mother's choice, The Philadelphia College of Art, located on Broad Street in Philadelphia. To her delight, as she waited at the train station to catch the train into town, her friend, Susan, from art class, was waiting there too and they rode in together, learning the 'underground' route that would lead them beneath the streets almost all the way to the school, saving them, in the long term, from rain and snow.

The underground was brightly lit, with mostly white tiled walls reflecting the light. Poster—advertisements for everything from cigarettes to airlines—lined the walls as well. There was, at one point, even a small kiosk offering magazines and candy. The underground passageway ran from about two blocks away from the school all the way to 30th Street Station.

The school, which sat on Broad Street, not far from City Hall and its well-known Billy Penn statue, presented an imposing façade, but the façade was the only imposing thing about the school. The wide, high-ceilinged front hall was clean, with dark marble tiled flooring and a reception area that led to long hallways on either side that led to classroom areas. The hallways were 'paneled' with homasote board, a grey cellulose-based fiber wall board about ¾ of an inch thick that was exceedingly convenient for pinning things to and absorbed sound to some degree. The two hallways flanked a long, open, grassy area below, often filled with lounging or lunching students, that could be seen through numerous windows. Each hall led to classrooms and stairways that led to classrooms on the upper levels. The classrooms that were right there, just off the first-floor hallways, were usually reserved for academic classes, like art history, while most of the studio spaces were either up or downstairs from there.

In the Freshman year at PCA, all students were required to take a sampling of classes so that they could get a taste of the wide variety of options that were offered. There were crafts, like weaving and pottery, as well as fine arts, like painting and sculpture, as well as commercially oriented classes, like fabric design, illustration, and industrial design. Happily, the new students were shepherded around for a day or two to learn the layout.

That first day was a long one. Mouse and Susan were exhausted by day's end, but as they made their way back to 30th Street Station, they connected with three other students they'd seen in classes that day and they all ended up on the same train at the same time almost every evening from then on. Mouse, Susan, Bill, Steven, and Gary had fun together and lived relatively close to each other. All were pretty much on the same footing—new kids in a new place—that they soon began hanging out together to watch the very campy television show "Batman" on a regular basis every Wednesday night. They called themselves "The Bat Gang."

Gary, who dressed a lot like a Philadelphia bus driver, seemed to be a never-ending source of information about all sorts of things and Mouse, by nature curious about pretty much everything, loved to listen to him explain about trains and scheduling and electronics... not that she understood most of it, she just liked hearing about it. She would take in volumes of information that she would never remember for the sheer joy of listening.

Gary must have taken note of her rapt attention and eventually asked her if she'd like to go to the movies some night. She said that she would, and they arranged a time for him to pick her up at the castle, as he lived not too far away.

Mouse was a tad surprised when her date showed up in a Maserati. She was a little disappointed that her father hadn't been home for this, but she slid happily into the passenger's seat when Gary opened the door for her. Her next surprise came when she found herself entering a movie theater that was showing Mary Poppins. She hardly knew what to make of it. Her father had introduced her to foreign movies before she was even in her teens and she was used to far headier stuff than this... that said, it was enjoyable enough.

As Gary dropped her off, he made no attempt whatsoever to kiss her, which she was thrilled about as she wasn't physically attracted to him at all; she just liked him as a person. He invited her out to his parent's place the following weekend. They could spend Saturday together; she could meet his sister and his parents.

No reason not to, she figured, and the date was confirmed. He lived in the area where "The Bat Gang" met, so she knew where to go as they'd all been taken for a wild ride on his family's property on some kind of four-wheeled vehicle once. Still, she'd not been in the house before and was a little confused as to where to park when she drove down the long driveway where he'd told her that she'd see the door to his room on her left.

She saw it, no problem there, but she was still on a driveway that obviously continued for some distance ahead. She stopped and went to knock on the inconspicuous door. Gary appeared and directed her to a place to park just a little farther down.

As she turned back toward her car, she caught sight of an obviously frequently used small target just opposite the door on which she'd knocked, just on the other side of her car. She stared at it. Gary, she sensed, was behind her, so she turned to him and, with an obviously questioning and possibly somewhat shocked look on her face, pointed wordlessly at the target.

"Target practice," he responded.

But from where, exactly, she wondered... *and across a driveway?*

With the question in mind, she proceeded to park her car and returned cautiously to the door, where Gary stood waiting to explain the setup.

There was a flood light over the door, he pointed out. Then, from a bedside table, he pulled out a cowboy-looking gun, replete with a carved ivory handle and signaled her to come into the room. His manner was that of a father explaining how a toilet might work to a small child. He motioned for her to stand behind him and cover her ears, which she did. He then took a shot at the target. It was entirely too loud for Mouse, who cringed.

"Sorry," he responded, looking genuinely concerned. Mouse nodded a wounded-looking "OK."

"I have ears like a bat," she explained. They sat and talked for a while. This was particularly nice for Mouse as she was more used to being drawn into make-out sessions and Gary wasn't anyone she wanted to make out with. She liked him, but with every passing moment, it was clear that he'd only be a friend.

Then she heard more gunshots, farther away this time, thankfully. She looked at Gary tentatively. Clearly oblivious to her somewhat nervous and uncomfortable state, he said, "Oh, that's my parents. They're skeet shooting. You ever shoot skeet?"

Feeling as if all she wanted to do at this point was get back in her car and leave, she instead slowly shook her head *no*.

Again, clearly unable to read any kind of a clue, he grabbed her hand, pulled her up, and trotted out his door. They walked a little farther down the drive, past her now parked car, as the offending bursts of gunshot grew louder. Mouse longed for earmuffs or, better yet, a get-away car.

Ahead, she could soon see what looked like a long, low, wooden counter with some sort of hardware on it...

this was called "the trap field," she would discover. There were established positions for the shooters. One shooter was already there, and more people soon came filing out of the upper level of the house, each taking a spot along the trap field. Gary introduced everyone to Mouse, then introduced Mouse to the technique. Even with protective ear-muff sorts of things, she lasted all of one round and begged off.

Clearly, this was not a match made in heaven. Gary and Mouse came from two different worlds, both were moneyed, but their culture was very, very different. They stayed friendly throughout freshman year when the curriculum and schedule were the same for everyone, but once the year was done, they saw each other rarely.

Mouse took up with one of the handsome and philosophic chess players whose mother was renting the carriage house on Gary's parents' property. He was a motorcycle-driving n'ere'do well who lived with his mother and thirty-some Pomeranian dogs.

She'd met another interesting young man in the cafeteria one day, though, with whom she would often find herself deeply engaged in conversations that spanned the spectrum from music to philosophy to advertising and onward. His name was John. Perhaps sensing that Mouse was an innately curious being and willing to think outside the box, he invited her to accompany him one day to the home of a friend of his, a woman named Jean, who shared her home with numerous other students as a means of paying the rent.

It was a much larger house than Mouse had expected to see and upon entering, she found that it also smelled different from anything she had ever smelled before. It was a not-unpleasant scent and smelled as if it might be some sort of incense, so she commented on it. It was, John informed her, the smell of an herb called marijuana that was being smoked somewhere in the house. The name rang a warning bell for her; she'd heard of it; it was illegal; she was uncomfortable with that and said so, but her new friends calmed her down by explaining that since they were all in a house, not out and about, causing a scene, that they were highly unlikely to be discovered. She exchanged glances with John, who nodded gently, his head tilted slightly to one side, reassuring her that Jean was right; there really was very little danger involved.

They settled down with Jean in the living room, where she had been doing something called "doing a reading" for someone. Unusual-looking cards with pictures of people wearing what looked might be medieval garb were arranged in a sort of pattern on the floor and a young woman, obviously waiting for Jean's return, sat on the floor by them. Mouse and John had taken to the couch, but Jean settled herself on the floor by the cards and Mouse watched as the "reading" unfolded.

Oh, my heavens, she thought to herself. *These must be the kinds of cards the Gypsies used! That's how they could tell the future. There's lots more to see here.* She made a mental note to look for tarot cards the next time she was in a bookstore. She'd been in a lot of bookstores but had never noticed anything like that... still, they must be somewhere. She'd find them, or a book about them, or something.

Her favorite bookstore was not far from the college. They sold used books at very good prices, and she had found a couple of books on astrology that she could easily afford. They didn't have anything, as it turned out, on tarot, though, so, on a hunch, she decided to cross the street and look in Wanamaker's to see if, perhaps, they had something. They did. But the prices were more than she could pay... thus began a brief period of stealing a few books from Wanamaker's because it turned out to be just so darn easy. She was a student; she was already carrying books; one or two more weren't going to be that obvious. She obtained the books she felt she needed and that was that.

Meanwhile, back at the castle, a new resident had moved in, Uncle Jack! Mouse was curious, upon coming home one day, to discover her mother escorting an elderly, and perhaps somewhat crippled, man, seeming to lend him support as he shuffled along. He didn't look entirely well, and he didn't look at all familiar. Polly was in the process of helping him navigate the oddly configured steps up to the front door.

Mouse hung back, not wanting to complicate the situation, and finally walked around to the kitchen door and through the kitchen in order to escape to her third-floor retreat. When she came down to dinner that night, she discovered that her usual seat—at the right-hand side of her father—(Polly sat at the left)—had been reassigned to the elderly man she'd seen that afternoon. Then she was introduced to her Uncle Jack in the flesh. She was delighted. It was like having a childhood dream come true. She imagined that this would be a permanent shift and that was just fine with that because it meant that she would get to be near Uncle Jack, whose very existence had fascinated her for so long.

Since Memo was the center of attention by design, it meant that she could also have the opportunity of observing her uncle as he ate. Knowing that Uncle Jack was unlikely, if not actually unable, to notice her furtive surveillance, she watched him as he maneuvered the silver, guiding what seemed like very small portions of food toward his mouth. He was slow and shaky but relatively accurate, though there'd be a little leakage at the corner of his mouth from time to time.

She admired him... his persistence, his acceptance of who he was, as he was, and his seeming comfort with that.

About two weeks after his arrival, though, when she went down to dinner, Uncle Jack was not there. She thought that perhaps he'd had to go to the hospital and asked no questions. She'd learned long ago when to ask questions and when to quell her curiosity; she could feel that this was one of those times when she needed to go on as if nothing out of the usual routine had changed.

After dinner, though, as she was loading the dishwasher with her mother—the help was always released from their work after their dinner—she asked the question she'd been sitting with since dinner. "Where's Uncle Jack? Is he OK?"

"I took your uncle to the train station this morning. He's gone back home."

"Oh," Mouse paused, "I thought he was going to stay with us now."

"He was," her mother sighed, "but your father couldn't stand to watch him eat."

Mouse took in a quick deep breath… not quite a gasp, but audible. Her mother went right back to her task but Mouse, her eyes filled with tears, turned away until she could compose herself since she had been forbidden to cry.

Daddy stopped coming at night. That was okay with Mouse because she was still his favorite. It was as if she could do no wrong. On one occasion, a year or so later, when he and Polly had taken a few of the sibs away for what was supposed to be a weekend at the house on the bay, a bad storm had strongly suggested that they head back home.

Back at the castle, where Mouse had been left in charge for the weekend, nobody knew anything about a storm and Mouse had taken advantage of her parent's absence by 'borrowing' Daddy's car—aka The Porsche—so that she could show off in front of her boyfriend's friends. Because she thought she could, because she thought that no one would ever know, she spent the night away at John's house because his mother was also away.

She'd headed home in the morning and gasped when she saw the VW sitting under the porte-cochere. She was in for it. Her brothers and sisters knew she had been away and when they'd heard the Porsche pull up, they'd positioned themselves discretely around the entrance to the master suite in order to be able to hear Mouse catch hell. She was barely breathing when she gently pushed the door in and peeked around the edge.

Memo didn't say a word... just signaled with his index finger that she should come in. Cautiously she entered, standing, facing him directly as he lounged back against the padded headboard. He made eye contact.

She took a sharp breath in.

"For God's sake, Mouse," he said softly but sternly, "be discreet. Take the station wagon."

The breath left her body. It was OK. She inhaled deeply, nodded, and left the room as her siblings attempted to flee unnoticed. What everyone in the house had taken for granted was now officially official. If that could happen, the Mouse could get away with murder in plain sight... but all she ever really wanted was love and her freedom... and books.

Looking For Help

When she'd been a senior in high school, Mouse had begun having dreadful dreams of rape and human sacrifice. They felt as real as life. She'd had other dreams as well, about her father lurking outside the bedroom window on the terrace that was there, wanting to have sex with her. She hated the dreams and didn't want to be having them, having far too successfully banished any conscious memories of incest and rape to a part of her mind that was inaccessible to her in waking life. She asked her mother if she knew a psychiatrist who might help her... and her mother did, she said, a friend of theirs who had an office in Philadelphia. She made an appointment for her daughter.

Mouse drove to the appointment, met with the doctor, and explained to him what was happening.

His immediate response was, "Oh, you shouldn't worry about that; all little girls dream about having sex with their fathers. Perfectly normal."

End of story. Bye bye.

Mouse sat in her car and, recognizing that she was too furious to drive, took deep breaths until she calmed down and then drove home, wishing that she'd never brought it up. Surely, he would be reporting back to Mommy and that would be the end of that. Except that it wasn't. The really bad dreams—the ones about human sacrifice—babies, really... brown babies, specifically—continued.

And she remembered a stressful moment that had occurred when she was very young. She'd been out shopping with her mother and Nana. They'd taken her into a toy store so she could get a treat and she had fallen in immediate love with a brown So-Wee Baby doll.

She brought the doll up front to where her mother and grandmother were waiting for her and handed the doll to her mother, telling her that that was what she wanted. Nana was, for reasons Mouse couldn't even have imagined, psychologically distanced as she was from everything that had gone on when she and Annie were in the woods, why Nana was so worked up.

For whatever reason, though, Polly came through for her daughter and the doll became her treasure.

About a year after the unpleasant incident with her mother's psychiatrist friend, the psychology class teacher at the college invited in a professional to talk with the class about inspiration and dreams and the power of images. He had brought with him a series of large inkblots which, as part of his presentation, he would hold up in front of the class, calling on different members of the class to say what each "saw" in the inkblot to illustrate how differently people can see things.

He called on Mouse. She reported that what she saw in that particular, horizontally positioned inkblot was a kind of rack like duck-hunters use to carry the ducks they've shot, but this one, she elaborated, was strung across a fence kind of a thing and what was hanging on it were burned, dead babies.

At the end of class, as the students were dispersing, the guest lecturer approached Mouse.

"I hope I'm not overstepping my bounds," he asked gently, "but are you engaged in any kind of therapy at the moment?"

Mouse reported that she was not, withholding the fact that she desperately wanted to be.

"It's something you might want to consider..." he added tentatively.

Mouse could only nod *yes,* and sigh.

That incident, though, gave her the courage to re-approach and plead with her mother again for the help. This time her mother recommended someone she knew from the hospital where she worked. Mouse would have to take the bus from the college to a stop that was about five blocks from the hospital, which was in a notoriously bad neighborhood, and she could walk to his office from there.

Mouse, it should be noted, generally liked to be noticed. The temperatures were running the high 80s and she was enchanted by mini shirts and bell-bottoms and culottes and outrageous colors, and she was going to an art school... whatever anyone wore, it was all fine there. The art school was on Broad Street, only blocks from City Hall; the hospital where her mother worked was in North Philadelphia and was nowhere near as commercial an area. Mouse had given no thought whatsoever to the kind of attention that she might generate in a so-called bad neighborhood, but she hadn't walked more than a block from where she had gotten off the bus before she found out.

She'd dressed that day in a short, full skirt that consisted of panels of purple, fuchsia, green, and yellow, all of which were polka dotted. Her top, which was black, like the polka-dots, was skin-tight. She was small-breasted, but there they were, on display.

A local high school happened to be letting out at about the same time she'd exited the bus and before she even realized what was happening, she had been surrounded by a group of boys who thought that it would be fun to torment her and began playfully shoving her around and across a closed circle created by their arms. She attempted to keep walking, pretending that she was ignoring them, which was impossible. She felt like a rag doll, and she was terrified. With the kind of luck that she would often seem to have, a police car rolled by slowly and she screamed out. Her scream was acknowledged by the sound of a siren and the boys dispersed in all directions as if they'd been sprayed with mace. Mouse got a ride to the hospital.

The visit with the psychiatrist, though, went badly. Noticing her obvious nervous state, he inquired as to what might have upset her. When she told him, he responded that she should really stop making this stuff up and that it was clear that she just wanted attention because... well... look how she was dressed. And he dismissed her.

She was furious but relieved as well to find the same police car parked outside. Hoping that the policeman had perhaps been waiting for her, she walked over and tentatively knocked on the window. Concerned for her safety, he *had* been waiting for her and drove her to the bus stop.

She could have gotten off the bus near the train station and gone straight home, but she was still angry with her mother and with her mother's doctor friends and she was frustrated as well that no one believed that she was having dreams that were relentlessly and genuinely frightening her. So, she stayed on the bus for another few blocks because she knew that one of her friends was having a party that night. She'd never been to a party in town, where so many of the students lived in small apartments or shared townhouses.

The townhouse was dimly lit, but the sound of music could be heard in the street. Never having attended anything like this before, she was feeling a bit overwhelmed, but tentatively she pushed open the door and followed the sounds of celebration. She peeked into the downstairs living room, saw no one that she recognized, and so made her way back toward the kitchen from which a great deal of intermingled conversations could be heard. A couple of her male friends from school were there and welcomed her in with obvious pleasure. She took the drink that was offered to her gladly and glanced around, hoping for some food. There was more drink than food available and in no time at all, she was feeling tipsy. This was a first. She'd had sips of her father's martinis at home and beer too, but she'd never had a whole drink all to herself. She was underage, but so were most of the people there.

She chatted with a few of her friends and then figured that she'd better get home. It was growing dark. She approached one of her classmates whom she knew also rode the train and asked if he'd mind walking her to the station. He seemed glad to do it and she was grateful as she was feeling very, very unsure of her footing.

They got on the train together and, fortunately, as he got off at the same stop as she, he offered her a ride home which she accepted very gratefully as, by then, night had fallen. As they drove into the driveway, she could see that the billiard room was lit up. *They must have company,* she thought and saw a chance to sneak in and up to her room without being caught in a state of mild drunkenness. That would not be good. Her friend dropped her off at the front of the house, where she attempted to enter unobserved, trying not to make any noise, but, of course, her parents had seen an unexpected vehicle approach and her mother met her at the door. It took her no more than a moment to discern the obvious and, in a loud whisper, dispatched her to her bedroom "pronto!"

This felt like a reprieve because it was. Mouse was quiet and quick and grateful and gone. The incident was never mentioned again. Her mother knew, and she knew, that this was the second time she'd been out when she should have been in. There'd be no more reprieves; there'd be grounding, a term Mouse had heard mentioned by her friends and was desirous of avoiding.

College was, for Mouse, the best of life that she had known thus far. She'd made friends of all sorts and was able to do what she loved. So, she was vastly disappointed when summer break came along to discover that her mother had arranged for her to have a summer job as an au pair. Every summer at the castle so far, she'd been able to make use of the nearby swim club where she mostly just "laid out," getting the kind of tan that Cuban girls get, deep and dark and brown... and surreptitiously eyeing the 50-something man in the red Speedo that was there every afternoon. She was being eyed, in turn, by more than a few young men, but they didn't interest her much; she just tanned and read. But there'd be no ogling older men that summer and she was beyond disappointed at her prospects until she discovered that the job was at the shore and that she was being given a Honda 50 motorbike to get around on.

Learning the bike was a bit challenging, though... and a great surprise, one morning, to her neighbors down the street as she lost control of it on a turn, jumped the curb, and zipped perilously close to the glass-enclosed breakfast room where a casually dressed family had been enjoying their morning meal. She was up the small hill, past the window, looking briefly at their startled faces, and gone in a flash, ruining only a little bit of lawn in the process. She never looked back.

Her summer job down the shore was in Ventnor, New Jersey and things were not as dismal as they had seemed they might be. The family—consisting of a grandmother, her daughter, who was the mother of two, and the father of the children, a lawyer who came in from Philadelphia to spend weekends. The mother did most of the work with the kids and Mouse's main job was to keep an eye on them at the beach. In keeping with a song that had been popular some years before, she'd gotten herself a polka-dot bikini—blue, with green dots—for beachwear. And, while the beach was mostly filled with moms and their kids, there were also lifeguards whose main activity seemed to be scanning for mothers' helpers. Mouse got noticed.

Mouse got so noticed that she got a few Saturday night dates out of it and then, much to her surprise, and probably because she was no stranger to sex, she was nominated by the crew to be a contestant in the Miss Ventnor pageant, one of the many pageants that lead up to the renown Miss America pageant. Her host family, having no idea, of course, about what Mouse did on her nights off, was tickled.

The week just prior to the event, Mouse was out and about on her Honda 50 when fate stepped in the form of two elderly folks who seemed to her to have jumped out from between two parked cars right in front of her and her motorbike, and down they all went.

Police were called, names were taken, and everyone was let go. Neither of the old folks had sustained even a scratch. Mouse, however, had been relieved of much of the skin on her upper right arm when the bike went down. A very thoughtful and nicely built young man who claimed to know a bit about dressing a wound invited her up to his meager summer flat, which consisted of a bed that was little more than a cot, a bathroom, and a television. He apologized for its condition; he was a law student just crashing here for the weekend. He pulled out a first aid kit, bandaged her arm, and then they had sex because they both found each other attractive. Invigorated, Mouse got back on the Honda and drove back to her employer's home with a little bit of explaining to do regarding her condition.

It wasn't until she was resting in bed that evening that she realized that she had a problem. She had a pageant to be in the following week and her right arm looked as if she'd leaned against a barbecue. What she needed, she realized, was a bathing suit with sleeves... but did such a thing exist? It must. She spent her day off going from one expensive boutique to another because she knew that if such a thing existed, it would be a specialty item because who in their right mind would want a bathing suit with sleeves? As the day was winding down, she finally found one. It was very simple, very elegant, and very expensive. It cost her all the money she had, but it was that or let down the Lifeguard crew that had honored her by giving her this opportunity.

When the night of the pageant came, Mouse was the only contestant in a swimsuit with sleeves. So unusual an event was that, apparently, when it came time for the Q&A session in front of the live audience, that was what the inquirer asked her about. There was no getting around it, though, and she wasn't going to lie. She'd had an accident, falling off her little motor bike, she said. There were audible gasps from the audience.

Oh well. She knew she hadn't had a chance anyway. She was the only brown-skinned person in the room, let alone in the contest. Mouse always looked like a native Cuban in the summertime. She loved the look and wished she could be that dark all year long, but by October, her skin would return to what her mother termed "olive," but amidst a bevy of lightly toasted blondes, she was clearly the odd one out.

Except for a furtive sexual affair with a mechanic she'd encountered post-accident, the rest of her summer was as dull as could be expected, keeping an eye on the kids and reading. Her parents came to pick her up on the appointed day in late August and, if nothing else, she returned home with new confidence in her motor-bike riding skills and looked forward to attempting the trip to school in Philly on her own.

Her newfound confidence, however, was immediately put in check when she was passed by a tractor-trailer. She was terrified most of the way into town and in no way looking forward to the trip home, which went wrong in a way she'd never expected as she ran out of gas on the crest of a lengthy suspension bridge that was a part of the Philadelphia Expressway and had to walk herself and her bike to the nearest gas station, which was not near at all. She returned home chastened by the incident and somewhat less in love with her small vehicle.

Rape

Mouse returned to train-commuting. Late one afternoon, as she de-boarded the train, a pleasant-looking man approached her and asked her if she'd like a ride home. He said that he'd seen her on the train before and passed her home on the way to his and would be glad to drop her off. Glad for the opportunity and not giving a second thought to the fact that he'd mentioned knowing where she lived, she accepted his offer. As they pulled away from the station, he began telling her, having noticed her portfolio, she guessed, that his wife was an artist... part-time, of course, he said, and told her that he thought his wife would enjoy talking to her about art school... could she spare some time to drop by their house before he took her home?

She didn't know him, but he was a neighbor; she made the mistake of trusting him. He did, indeed, live nearby. His house was one of the more ordinary-looking houses that made up the neighborhood, and the kitchen they entered was a typical-looking kitchen. He called out a name—Mouse would never remember what name—as if he were really expecting her to be there. He waved back toward Mouse, signaling for her to follow him into the living room. It all seemed perfectly normal. He pointed out one of his wife's supposed paintings hanging over the fireplace. It was a landscape, a watercolor, pretty but ordinary. The next thing she knew, there was a knife at her throat and one of her arms was being held in a very tight grip.

"Don't try to get away," he cautioned with a vicious edge to his voice.

She was terrified to even move, let alone make a break for it. Pulling her by the arm, he roughly guided her to the bedroom, where he threw her to the bed as he cautioned her not to resist... or else. He put the knife on a headboard sort of shelf that was above and behind her head. It was a sort of knife such as she had never seen before; it was shortish, with a thick, curved handle and had a wide blade.

The childhood rapes in the woods came back to her... she left her body... she sort of hovered above herself, watching as the man yanked off her panties and penetrated her roughly, saying things aloud, she couldn't tell what. The next thing she knew, he was throwing her panties at her, shouting instructions, and threatening her life if she ever said anything.

Speechless and terrified, she did as she was told.

Yanking her by her right arm, he pulled her from the bed and semi-dragged her back through the house to the kitchen door and down the steps to his car, glancing around as he did. He took her to the passenger side and warned her to act "normal" as he opened the door for her. Mouse got in, sat down, said nothing, and could only hope that this time, he would actually take her home.

"You ever tell anyone about this..." he said in a threatening tone, leaving the sentence and its implications hanging mid-air.

He drove the two blocks to the entrance of the driveway to the castle and did not even turn to look at her as he commanded, "Get out."

He pulled away the moment she was clear of the car. She stood there, shaking, wanting to pull herself together before going into the house lest the help noticed the state she was in. Upstairs, safe in her room, unseen by anyone, she collapsed, feeling as if she couldn't even breathe, let alone cry. By dinnertime, the terror had almost gone, but she would carry the memory for as long as she lived.

Help?

There was a problem with keeping help in the castle. Minding 11 "children," some of whom are beyond "minding" age, keeping doctors and dentist appointments, food shopping, preparing meals, plus the upkeep demanded by a "house" that size was a bigger job than, perhaps, than most folks realized it might be.

Fred and Ethel had lasted barely a year. Polly tried "day" help, figuring that she could perhaps leave a chastened Mouse to oversee week-ends while she and Memo escaped to the shore house, but the 100+ people party that had just seemed to kind of "fall together" one weekend while her parents were away, and the fact that her father's Emperor-sized bed—that's two king mattresses side-by-side—had clearly been the scene of something orgy-like one week-end ended that, so live-in help was again sought.

There was one young and very attractive couple from Belgium that stayed for a while. None of the kids was very disappointed when they had left... it was the one dinner that pushed almost everyone over the edge: Marie Jean, the wife, had pressed raw ground meat of some sort into a large Jello mold and decorated it with a couple dozen small, curved gherkins, all pointing up like miniature spires on a castle. There was the usual limp salad and a cooked vegetable, of course... and everyone was required to "have a helping" of the "steak tartare" and at least "take a taste." Memo and Polly seemed to have no problem with it, but there was much subdued muttering around the table. Everyone knew better than to fuss loudly.

That couple didn't last very long. Neither did the ex-Vietnam vet and his wife, but that may have had more to do with their overall lack of interest in doing anything at all. The wife's younger brother, however, had taken a keen interest in the Mouse, as she had in him, and that discovery may also have contributed to the end of their term of employment.

It was back to dayworkers. Eventually, Mouse became the de facto food shopper and cook and pretty much everything else was left to fend for itself. Meanwhile, she and her friend, John, had become more than friends. He lived in his own apartment... one floor up from his parent's apartment, in the Philadelphia suburbs. Life in your own place looked pretty pleasant to her and she began to imagine how she might manage to make that happen. Her mother had begun badgering her about taking a job on the weekends and she thought that, perhaps, that was the way to go. Certainly, it would provide her with some sort of an income. She had no idea how much money she would have to come up with to be able to move out, but she set about exploring her options and decided that the weekend job was probably a good place to start. Since she wasn't trained in any particular skill, becoming a "shop girl" seemed as if it might be something that she could do and could possibly get hired to do. She decided to start at one of her mother's favorite stores, Lord & Taylor and, to her surprise, she got hired.

Mouse was no salesgirl, but she was an attractive physical presence who looked good in clothes and so she got by, writing up the occasional sale and keeping both the stock and the stock room in order, both of which jobs she discovered that she enjoyed more than working with people. She also discovered, upon one day being asked to take a garment that had met with something unpleasant to the dry cleaners, that it would be easy to steal clothes that way. She didn't do it a lot because most of the clothes they had were far too conservative for her, but she did manage to dry clean a few items that never made it back to the store.

Once summer came, she began working full-time. Eventually she'd gotten together enough money—or so she thought—to scope out a possible apartment for herself in town. While she was disappointed time and time again by the actual costs, she finally came across a fourth-floor walk-up on the ragged edge of what had once been a very fashionable part of Philadelphia. The rent was $75 a month. She would have to figure in bus fare to the suburbs for her job as well since she didn't own a car and her parents had sold the Honda not long after the running-out-of-gas-on-the-bridge debacle. She put down her first month's rent, got the keys and returned to the castle to borrow her mother's credit card briefly in order to stock her apartment with needed non-perishable items and put a down payment on a telephone. Then, one day, she left for work and never came home.

Not realizing, or simply not thinking far enough ahead, it had never occurred to her that her parents might not be paying for her continued college education. Thus, it was that she became a full-time shop-girl. Thus, it also was that she soon found herself existing on peanut butter sandwiches and canned vegetables. But she still had a boyfriend and he'd invite her over to his place on a Saturday and they'd have dinner with his parents, so she'd have at least one tasty meal a week. *His parents,* she thought, *were a bit odd.* They had a small dog, but they didn't prefer to take it for walks, so a few times a day, they'd put it in the bathtub, where it had learned to relieve itself. Aside from that, they seemed... old. Mouse's parents never seemed old to her. It made her think... what makes some people old and others, who are the same age, not? She would still be wondering that when she, herself, was in her 70's.

While the apartment Mouse had sufficed to keep her off the streets, it was a very minimal sort of residence, consisting of a large space that had likely once served as a living room but was now partitioned by a half-wall/countertop near the entrance. If, after entering the space, you immediately turned to your right, you'd have been facing a small sink that stood about six feet away. To the left, on the countertop, was a hotplate, and to its right, a small refrigerator. She couldn't afford television and there was none in the room, so she read a lot, novels mostly.

The front room had two long narrow windows that looked out to the townhouses across the street. There was one very large, low, ancient-looking dresser against the entry-side wall and a surprisingly small closet—only about eight inches deep—on the opposite wall. The bathroom was also small... very small. The sink, which one encountered immediately to the right of the door upon stepping into the space, was equally small, it had to be. The shower stood... no, hung, really, about a yard ahead. It consisted of an overhead showerhead attached to a pipe and a drooping metallic loop that sported a not-very-clean-looking shower curtain. Every time a bus or large truck passed by on the street below, the entire apparatus shook.

A toilet sat between the sink and the shower and, directly across from it, just below the juncture of wall and ceiling, there was a small, rectangular, metal-framed window that could only be either all the way opened or all the way closed

When summer came around Mouse found herself missing out on the shore house and, perhaps even more so, missing out on getting tan. She loved being brown, as opposed to being "olive." Olive was in-between and apparently confused some people. Most of the white people she'd known had ranged from catty to inhuman, while most of the brown people she'd known had been taking care of her, so her viewpoint was skewed, but she was young and kind of an idiot. She liked making a statement, though, and she preferred brown. John had a sunlamp. He brought it over to her place one night and showed her how to use it.

That weekend she spent Sunday afternoon sunning herself while reading a paperback. As night began to fall, her eyes began to hurt and then burn, and then she began to have difficulty seeing. Panicked that she had somehow blinded herself, she overcame her fear and called home. Probably only because of the lateness of the hour, her father—whom she had never seen answer a phone—picked up.

"Daddy?" she hazarded weakly, knowing the kind of trouble she must be in with her parents, what with having taken and used their credit card so liberally.

He must have heard the fear in her voice, though, for he responded, "Mouse, are you OK?"

All she could do was cry. He remained quiet, listening, waiting.

"I think I burned my eyes," she sobbed. "I was using a sunlamp…" she began.

"But you *can* see?" he hazarded.

"Yes… but… not well."

"Tell me where you are," he said. "And try to get some sleep. I'll be there in the morning."

Only the potent combination of emotional exhaustion and fear allowed her to sleep. When Memo arrived, he checked out her eyes and breathed a sigh of relief as they seemed to be not too damaged. He prescribed gentle eye washing and a lot of rest, eyes closed. He called her in sick, then called John, who, by then, had become her official boyfriend, for her so that she could make arrangements to have him take her to his apartment where she could both rest peacefully and have help available if she needed it.

Then he asked her if she would consider moving home and returning to school in the fall. Without a moment's hesitation, she agreed. She'd missed a year and wasn't sure what that would mean for her, but she hadn't chosen a major yet and she'd have to make up her mind about that before she re-applied. Something deep inside her relaxed and after her father left, and she fell back asleep.

Picking Up Where She Left Off

Mouse did not have to spend too long at John's apartment as her eyes healed more quickly than she'd imagined they would. She then returned home to her former role as procurer and preparer of food. The college accepted her back, but she had to pick up where she left off, having missed an entire year of classes.

She also had to decide upon a major... there was so much to pick from. Freshman year had been all about getting a taste of this and that, and there were certain programs that she knew she wouldn't be taking. "Clay class" was one of those. Her skills at producing three-dimensional objects—figurative or useful, like cups or bowls—was non-existent. The pottery wheel was a dervish as far as she was concerned, the clay she was working with always seemed to have a mind of its own and inevitably ended up flying off the wheel. Illustration was boring—you had to develop a style and stick to it forever. Industrial Design involved mathematics and that was never a strong suit of hers. She loved printmaking but didn't quite know what to do with that as far as getting a job went. (She did steal a lot of type, though... it was just so pretty!)

Education was out of the question because anything to do with children was out of the question. She'd had enough of that at home. Her painting teacher, in her freshman year, had told her that she really belonged down the street, at The Academy of Fine Arts, that she was a painter, but she'd been to shows there; she'd seen the work those students produced, and she couldn't even imagine what her teacher was thinking. She knew she didn't have the kind of talent those students had. Their work amazed her. The only options left, then, were photography and fabric design and she decided on fabric design because she loved pattern. It was that simple. She had a sketchbook at home filled with all kinds of repetitive designs. She was obsessed with pattern from a drawing standpoint, so fabric design it was... there was only one problem... unlike most other majors, fabric design required an extra year. Why that extra year was necessary, exactly, she would never understand, but the department heads suggested to her that she could make it up by spending the summer at a place called Penland in North Carolina, where she could learn some of the weaving portions of the requirements.

It would cost extra, and she'd have to live there all summer, leaving her parents the task of replacing her as a shopper and chef. But, she figured, no harm asking... and much to her surprise, they agreed to it. The trip would also mean that she'd have to paint her car.

When she'd come home for her last birthday, they'd given her a partially paid-for Volkswagen beetle. It would be her responsibility to pay it off. This way, she could drive herself to school every day and not have to rely on the train. She'd painted the brown car, covering it from front to back and top to bottom in flowers, black and white, with variously colored centers. There was pretty much no way, she knew, that she could drive that car, painted like that, through the south and so, much to her dismay, she painted over it, returning it to its former neutral state.

Penland

The drive to North Carolina was the longest trip that Mouse had ever taken on her own and it was on roadways she'd never traveled. She was, understandably, nervous, driving her tiny brown bug amidst a sea of goal-oriented tractor-trailers, especially as, when they passed her at high speed, the bug would briefly be somewhat pushed aside.

Ultimately, she got where she was going, but once there, she didn't know where to go. There was no obvious office to be seen, so she pulled into the first parking area she saw where other cars were already parked, got out, and set off to find out what would happen next.

The campus was situated on gently rolling ground and dotted with wooden buildings of various shapes and sizes. None looked particularly office-like, so she finally approached one of the folks walking around, explained her situation, and was directed to the home of the people in charge, which was one of the many wooden structures that peppered the hillside.

The couple—a man and a woman—were in front of their home, engaged in play with what Mouse assumed was their child, when she approached. They saw her coming and began walking toward her with welcoming smiles on their faces. It seemed almost as if they'd been expecting her... and they had been alerted by the college that she'd be arriving that weekend. They introduced themselves and then directed her to where she'd be staying for the summer, in one of the many look-alike cabins. Her room was on the second floor and its small window faced the campus. There was a single bed pressed against the entry wall, a very basic, small bureau, and a wooden chair. It was enough. A deep sense of relief washed over her. She was there. She had a place to be. It felt good.

She'd passed a pay phone on the way in, so she gathered up some change and called home to let them know that she had been installed. A younger sister took the message and that was the last contact she had with her family for the summer. That, too, for reasons she could not pinpoint, also felt good.

Night fell, but through her open window, she could hear voices. This place apparently did not shut down at night. As she would discover, it never shut down. Any resident/student could visit the studio of their choice at any hour they wished, night or day. The instructors kept what might be called regular hours, but the facilities were left open and available right through the night.

Mouse slept well, having fallen asleep to the sounds of distant chatter.

Come morning, and an empty tummy, she realized that she hadn't inquired about food. She dressed and headed outside, confident that breakfast must be somewhere and, sure enough, it was. She noted that, from here and there, men and women of various ages seemed to be wandering across the grassy sloping land in one direction; she fell into the human wave and found herself at a very large lodge-looking kind of a place with a bank of windows where she could see enough heads and shoulders to determine that that's where breakfast was.

Inside was an arrangement such as she had never seen. Large, round tables filled the windowed area and each table had at its center a raised, smaller, round table-top-looking thing with bowls and small platters of food on it... and it rotated! She watched as people served themselves from the moveable serving tray. Amazing. You could take as much or as little as you like. Gentle chatter filled the room. It was... lovely.

After breakfast, Mouse made her way to the weaving room, which was in one of the many wooden structures sprinkled across the hillside. The weaving room happened to be just across the way from her room. It was immense, taking up the entire floor of the building. Skeins of yarn in what seemed like hundreds of colors hung from wooden pegs at one side of the room and most of the looms were already dressed and in use. One of the instructors approached her and upon seeing her mystified look, took her to an available loom and began to explain how to 'dress' a loom. It seemed pretty overwhelming, but it soon became clear that it was not really a complex process, just a painstaking one. It took her the rest of the day, with a break for lunch, to complete the task. Her next task would be that she would have to create a project based on the brilliant orange color she'd chosen to be the warp, which was the name for all the threads going from the front of the loom, where she'd be sitting, to the back. Tomorrow… the weft!

And tomorrow also, as it turned out, would be her introduction to natural dying and spinning. The woman who taught these skills had a log cabin set at some distance from the main campus. She also had three Samoyed dogs, a father and two sons. They may have been the reason that her little place—which barely held the dogs and her two spinning wheels—was set at some distance from the main campus, as every night, she let the dogs run loose. They were a magnificent—if eerie—sight under a fulling moon and also a bit daunting.

Under the tutelage of the woman who taught spinning and dyeing, Mouse would learn skills she would never use again, like creating dyes from wildflowers and grasses and using a spindle. But the atmosphere was one she would never forget. The class, like the weaving class, was made up entirely of women, and as part of a circle of women, stirring an immense cauldron filled with grasses and leaves and water with long, sturdy, stripped branches over an open fire, under a full moon, she felt like part of a coven. It was a strange feeling, an at-one-ment that ended the moment they left the place. They'd never even introduced themselves to each other. Clearly, some of the women knew others, but there was only, perhaps, about a dozen of them. Everyone followed directions and assisted each other with tasks, usually wordlessly. Even in the daylight, the place looked magical, with yarns of every imaginable color hanging out to dry on a clothesline that stretched from one porch post to another.

One night, after dinner, Mouse was drawn, as many of the students were every night, to the glassblowing area. It was a dramatic scene, with a line of glassblowers practicing and producing in the lights of glowing fires. The hot, glowing, liquid glass in its many colors was spellbinding. The glassblowers were manipulating, on the end of what looked like a long piece of pipe that they appeared to be blowing into, amorphous blobs of essentially liquid glass. It was the best show in town. The colors were brilliant and the failures dramatic.

One evening, as she walked from the glassblowers' row back toward her cabin, Mouse spotted a long-haired young man who seemed to be, at first glance, burying a piece of pottery. He was, as it turned out, using a special technique, something she'd not heard of in her brief time in the pottery studio in freshman year.

Raku is a technique potters use to make a glaze seem to shine with colors from within. The fired pieces are taken from the kiln while they're still glowing red hot and are then placed in a material that can catch fire, like sawdust or newspaper. This technique deprives the piece of oxygen, creating colors within the glaze. It was nowhere near the show that glassblowing was, but she was fascinated, nonetheless, and happened to have spent lunch at the same table as the young potter, who was more than happy, under the stars, to explain what he was up to.

His name was Eddie and he seemed... sweet. She'd never met a man that seemed sweet. She liked him. He fit the description of a hippie, with long, black curly hair that hung to his shoulders. Mouse was anything but a hippie, but in this environment, she was the one who didn't fit in... though no one seemed to care, including her.

Mouse, in fact, as she failed to remind herself, was not only not a hippie, she was also a clothes horse. What the '60s held for her was outrageous clothes and miniskirts and boots and being a go-go dancer for the Friday night dances at the college. She liked being the center of attention... but there was something about this place that she liked as well; she just didn't feel as if she were really a part of it. And this boy, Eddie, that's all she needed. She already had two boyfriends, one in Philadelphia and one in New England.

But those boyfriends weren't in North Carolina, so she and Eddie ended up right where you'd expect, in her bed. They were soon officially recognized—if not actually approved of—as a couple, His closest friends, gentle and intelligent post-hippie types, were concerned for him as they didn't entirely trust Mouse.

Come summer's end, Mouse invited Eddie to come and visit with her for a while. She was back at home again, with her own room and, by now, it was just accepted that she might be sleeping with someone. The visit didn't last long, though. Mouse had been able to make it through a summer in an environment that was, while lovely, totally foreign to her; Eddie had not been designed to be malleable in that way. Eddie was a hippie, and in an atmosphere fueled by image and self-centeredness, he was like a fish out of water. He didn't even last a week. He was very clear with her about why he was leaving, and she had seen the truth of it. They parted in agreement and sadness, and within a week, Mouse had made arrangements to visit her old boyfriend in New Hampshire, whom, despite her refusal to marry him, she was still connected to.

Annie

Mouse and Annie had shared a bedroom until Mouse had started college. Bedrooms, it seemed, were always being shifted in the castle. Annie, because of her accident, was two grades behind Mouse and had grown resentful of her older sister for reasons Mouse could not fathom. One day, as Mouse had been preparing to leave for school, checking herself out in the full-length mirror that lined the closet door, Annie shouted angrily at her from her bed, "You look like you always look," she snarled. "You look like a whore."

Mouse was taken aback. She was surprised, first of all, that her shy, younger sister even knew the word "whore," but was also stunned by being compared to one. She said nothing, went about gathering her things and left the room. She would have a new bedroom, all to herself, before the next day, but she was hurt and could not imagine why her younger sister seemed so angry.

Two years later, though, Annie was returned from the college she'd determined to attend, having been diagnosed as a delusional paranoid schizophrenic. Her delusions had a lot in common with the bad dreams that had sent Mouse in search of therapy, but Annie's delusions were, to her, as real as life itself. Men, she kept complaining to the police, were following her; they wanted to rape her; they were everywhere.

In addition to that, she had been reported to the police by the wife of one of the instructors, who had complained that Annie had been stalking her husband, which was true. Her husband had been the reason that Annie had chosen that particular college. She'd developed a crush on him in high school, where he'd been her art teacher, and when he left the high school to teach at the college level, she'd tracked him down and applied to the school when she graduated.

Back at home again, having nothing to do and no reason to stay home, Annie began taking the train into town and exploring the streets of Philadelphia. One day, she was approached by a young man wearing saffron robes who was begging for money. He began explaining his devotional practice to her. Down the block, she could see others who were similarly dressed. She walked among them and talked with them, and they invited her to return with them to their temple, which she did. They seemed kind and gentle.

The more she learned about the Hare Krishnas, the more she wanted to become one of them. The piece of information that sealed the deal was when she discovered that, in marriage, one could only have sexual relations for the purpose of creating another human being and even then, relations could only take place once a month.

That was the deciding point; she would join them. She would eventually marry within the sect, create one child, and then divorce, but she remained, for the rest of her life, "a devotee," living alone, supported by her mother, helping to care for the temple if she were near one. Mouse helped her out as much as she could, even taking her in for a while toward the end of her life, which she brought upon herself, refusing medical treatment for an infected wound.

Back To School... & Beyond

Mouse had returned to the Fabric Design department bearing her completed summer project: a poncho woven in neon colors—orange, yellow, pink, and green—with a decorative orange fringe and a more subtle green velveteen lining. These were colors that, before that day, had not been seen in the weaving department and the gasps from the instructors were audible. Nevertheless, she had met the challenge and her missed year was considered to have been made up.

Her last year at school would require, in place of a thesis, for the weaving department, the completion of a rug. For the dyeing and design department, though, the doors had been thrown wide open. It was all about an expression of imagination and creativity. So Mouse had constructed a model of an interior space utilizing dyed translucent fabric in place of walls. It was a fragile piece of mediocre worth, but it was done. Had she not successfully but narrowly avoided being part of a multi-car accident on the Benjamin Franklin bridge on the way in, the day of her presentation, she might have earned her usual B+, but all she had were crushed remains. She accepted the B she received and thanked them for their generosity and for being able to imagine.

Never one to stand on ceremony, she skipped graduation ceremonies altogether.

At winter break, Jerold had asked if he could visit. The last time she'd seen him had been in the fall. New England was a fabulous display of color in the fall, and they'd had a pleasant visit. She thought that she might not mind seeing him again so soon, but on the evening of his first night, in her bedroom in the castle, he'd presented her, as he sat on the edge of her bed, with an engagement ring which she refused… essentially twice, having already refused the offer alone on the yacht trip previously.

She'd seen him disappointed before, but she'd never seen him angry… and he was angry. He swore that he would never see her again and told her that he was going to throw the ring in the Schuylkill River. She looked straight at him but said not a word, at which point he rose and left and that was the last she ever saw of him.

She was officially down to one boyfriend: John. Now all she had to do was find a job. She knew, because the staff had been very up front about it, that just about the only place she could get a job utilizing the skills she had learned would be New York City. By extension, this meant that she'd have to move to New York City because that kind of daily commute wasn't an option, but the idea of living in New York terrified her. The idea of losing the dependable lifestyle to which she'd become accustomed also terrified her. She remembered her days in the walk-up on Sansom Street. Who could she call on for help in NYC? No one. She wasn't going. End of story.

Thus began a lengthy and depressing search of local mills, which were not in abundance and, for the most part, were far from thriving and not looking for additional help, though her persistence ultimately paid off at least a little. One of the mills maintained a small boutique shop not far from Rittenhouse Square, which was a decently plush area. Most likely because she was smartly dressed and attractive, the personnel manager mentioned that they had a sales position open at their store. It was a minimum wage job with a discount on personal purchases, but it was a job, and she was tired.

She showed up for work the next day and, within a few weeks, had seen the opportunities the tiny store provided for enhancing her wardrobe free of charge. She also noticed that the store's manager, who enjoyed her opportunities to take off any time she liked because now there was someone to mind the store, was none too discrete about funding her outings with the cash from the register. This would be a perfect spot.

The boutique was remarkably space-challenged. It was no more than four yards wide. Racks of clothes lined each of the side walls and another rack sat in the center of the floor.

Because the store catered to women in and around her age range, Mouse would occasionally get to socialize with old friends and acquaintances from as far back as high school. One of her old classmates worked about two blocks away in an upscale shoe store, so occasionally, Mouse would stop by her friend's place of employment to check it out. It was a fortunate happenstance as someone in accounting eventually detected a discrepancy between the received receipts for sales in the store and the actual money in the register. Her manager threw Mouse under the bus, fired her preemptively, and that was the end of that job. Mouse, knowing that she had been, in fact, guilty of occasional stealing, figured that it was best not to make a fuss and departed quietly.

She went straight from getting fired to putting in an application at the shoe store where her friend worked and was hired within the day. The store itself was magnificent, two stories high with a grand curving stairway to the second floor and the shoes were to die for. She very much enjoyed working with her old friend and much of their free time was spent catching up on the events of the years that had gone by since they'd last seen each other.

Sue, her friend, was in a relationship with a beautiful young man whom she very much loved. She also had, though, a very good friend named Paul, who was an art teacher and single. Mouse was longing for someone normal. Her last date—a customer who'd seemed nice enough—had ended with her fleeing from his apartment after he'd threatened to lock her in a closet if she didn't "put out."

Sue thought that Mouse and her friend might make a good match and invited him to the store one afternoon to meet her. He was a good-looking guy and seemed nice. It was toward the end of the day and so he invited her to join him for dinner at a nearby restaurant. He'd just blown his paycheck on a Pierre Cardin suit (she had to admire that), so it wouldn't be a fancy dinner, but they could get to know each other.

Not expected anywhere, Mouse agreed to his offer, and off they went to a small corner restaurant a few blocks away. Having been introduced to the joys—and safety—of something called layaway, Mouse was, in addition to her purse, toting a shopping bag containing three pairs of rather expensive shoes. As they were seated in a booth, she shoved the bag up against the wall and proceeded to peruse the menu. They ordered and chatted, exchanging basic life information till the food arrived. Not more than a few minutes after they'd been served, chaos ensued. Kitchen staff began pouring into the room from the back, where the kitchen was. Smoke rolled into the room from the back. Waitresses, carrying their handbags, were running through the restaurant, alerting patrons to the fire in the kitchen as they headed for the door. The staff was rapidly followed by the diners, including Paul and Mouse, who had been sitting relatively close to the front door. Sirens could be heard in the distance. Flames became visible.

Once safe on the pavement across the street, Mouse realized that she had left in such a hurry that she'd left her new shoes behind. She made an unconscious but audible sound of dismay. Paul reacted immediately, "What?" he asked. "What's wrong? Are you burned?"

"No... no," she replied resignedly. "I forgot to grab my shoes."

The look on his face was one of utter disbelief. "No!" he cried aloud and before she could utter a word, he rushed back toward the open door. Many of the people watching began yelling, telling him not to go back in. He didn't seem to hear them, and, in a flash, he was gone.

Mouse thought she might be sick, but in what seemed like seconds, he reappeared, carrying the unharmed bag of shoes, restoring it to her. He then walked her to the train station and, before they parted, asked her to join him for dinner the next week. She agreed readily, still somewhat in shock but definitely looking forward to it.

Currently, Mouse was occupying the front, left bedroom and turret in the castle with John. When she arrived home later than usual, she told him that she'd been out with friends and the restaurant had caught fire and that seemed like enough information to satisfy him. He had a job as well, so the two of them often found themselves passing each other, coming, or going. They were more like roommates with privileges at that point than like boyfriend and girlfriend. It was an arrangement that suited them both and was consciously ignored by the rest of the household.

Date night came and Mouse drove into town since, for the most part, traffic was all going the other way. She met Paul at the appointed restaurant and, over dinner, at some point, their eyes met and something very different from anything she'd ever experienced before happened. She couldn't wrap her head around it, couldn't put a word to it, but it almost felt to her as if he was looking into her soul... or something. It was mesmerizing.

They parted, agreeing to spend the next weekend together at his apartment, which was in Philadelphia. He took the address of the castle and the forewarning of its unusual appearance, and they parted.

The following Friday night, he arrived promptly. Mouse, her overnight bag packed, bid her mother farewell, said that she'd be back Sunday, and off they went to Paul's modest apartment on the outskirts of Philadelphia, in a tall, brick building not far from where John's apartment had been. The area was in the vicinity of Wissahickon Creek, and old trees grew everywhere. The building had an attached parking garage and elevators as well as stairs. Paul's apartment was a few floors up and didn't have much of a view considering the options, but they spent very little time looking out the windows.

It was a night she would remember for the rest of her life. She'd known that he was a painter, but she was not prepared for the level of skill his work exhibited. The work that hung on his walls was far and away the best 'student' work she'd ever seen... of course, he was a teacher, but the work had been produced while he'd been in college. One of the pieces, a small oil painting entitled The Immaculate Conception, was mind-blowing, an interpretation that would have scandalized most "good Christians," as the Virgin's face—which took up most of the surface—looked terrified. It was at once compelling and repulsive, and Mouse was more impressed by it than she had been since she'd first seen Prometheus Bound as a child.

In addition to his painting, also displayed were replicas of various medieval weapons, most of which looked exceedingly dangerous. This was the most interesting young man she had ever met. When she expressed interest in what she would soon learn was called a cross-bow, he took it down from the wall—it had been hanging in his bedroom—threw open the closet door, stepped to the other side of the room, cautioned her to stay where she was, and proceeded to shoot what she would learn was called the 'bolt'—a shorter, more sturdy version of an arrow, it seemed—into the far wall of the closet.

If she hadn't been impressed before, she was now. This guy was fascinating. Not too much later, they were in bed. Over the course of about the next eighteen hours, there were equal amounts of conversation and sex with a little local sight-seeing worked in. Then he asked her to marry him. She was shocked but also delighted and intrigued.

"Yes," she said without a moment's thought. Marriage. This would definitely be better than everything she'd been through. He was handsome; he was interesting; he was employed... and it might just serve to keep her out of trouble... What the hell? Why not?

"When I take you home," he said, "I'll ask your father for your hand."

Quaint, she thought, *but no harm in it, certainly.*

She smiled.

They arrived at the castle the next day, just at cocktail hour. The lights of the billiard room shone onto the side lawn as they drove in. *Perfect,* thought Mouse.

As she escorted Paul toward the billiard room, she took note of his eyes, scanning the wood paneling on the balustrade that linked the stairs to the second floor, the marble-fronted fireplace, the marble-floored dining room off to the left, the billiard table straight ahead.

As Mouse and Paul stepped down onto the one broad, tiled step into the billiard room, her parents greeted them, welcomed her home, and offered him a drink, which he declined. Then her father stepped out from behind the bar to shake hands and Paul got right down to it as soon as pleasantries had been exchanged.

"I came here tonight, sir, to ask your permission to marry your daughter."

Mouse had inhaled as he'd spoken and was still holding her breath when she heard her father's enthusiastic response. She was a little stunned, not so much by the "yes," she was used to her father allowing her pretty much anything she wanted, but by the enthusiasm, he'd displayed. He seemed positively thrilled.

Then, the reason for his seemingly unbridled joy came out.

"I am really going to enjoy telling that bastard upstairs—*(John)*—to get out of my house," he said, sounding genuinely gleeful as he walked toward the steps.

Mouse had been momentarily stunned by his words, but as he made his way toward the steps, she remembered that John probably *was* in her room. He'd been living there for months, with an exquisite sense of timing, coming and going as he pleased while managing to avoid contact with either of her parents.

A small parade, not including Paul, who was slightly mystified by whatever was going on, followed him: Mouse, her mother, and a sibling or two. Out of the billiard room, they went, up the front stairs, across the balustrade, up the next set of stairs, through the open hall, to the door that led to the third-floor quarters, up the stairs, and over to the door on the left.

He knocked.

John opened the door, looking somewhat startled as no one had ever knocked on the door before.

"Get out," her father said to him. "She's getting married."

John's sudden intake of breath was audible.

He nodded quickly and turned, without closing the door, to begin packing.

The parade turned itself around and went back to the bar for a celebratory round of drinks. John could be heard making his exit. Eventually, after more hand-shaking and some tentative plan-making, a date was set, Paul went home, and Mouse went off to bed pondering ideas for a wedding dress in a hurry because, for whatever reason, Paul wanted to marry quickly.

The Wedding

The date for the wedding was set for Valentine's Day evening, which was two weeks away. Plans were quickly made. Why there seemed to be such a rush around it was not clear. A few handwritten invitations were sent out, mostly to relatives. The wedding would be held at the castle, in the front hall. The reception, catered by a local restaurant, would be in the dining room. Their honeymoon would be at the small new shore house in Ocean City.

About two days before the wedding, Mouse came down with a fever and a cough that would have done a chain-smoking truck driver justice. She remained as horizontal as possible to absolutely no effect. So, on the morning of the wedding, her mother made a quick trip to the drug store, returning home with a clear liquid called ETH and C which was short for *elixir terpin hydrate codeine*, a cough suppressant sometimes referred to as "GI gin." Her instruction to her daughter was to sip it slowly throughout the day. It would be an evening wedding and one that Mouse would never remember. She could barely stand, let alone think.

The master of ceremonies was a local manure salesman who had gotten himself a mail-order ordination. On such short notice, he was all they could get. The ceremony was perfunctory; the food was OK, and Mouse had the obligatory dance with her father. Paul and she spent the night in her room and left for the shore house in the morning.

On their first night at the shore house, Paul took Mouse out to the movies to introduce her to pornography. *It was,* she thought, *possibly the least sexy thing she had ever seen, if not actually somewhat repulsive.* It was a black-and-white film that looked as if it might have been shot by someone who was new to the concept of filming... also scriptwriting. Having spent some time in her youth watching foreign films with her father in an art theater, she may have been a little spoiled, but Paul's concentration on the screen never flagged. She didn't quite know what to think and there was nothing to do but wait it out.

That night a snowstorm blanketed the upper east coast, causing the waters of the bay to rise. The couple awoke to discover water in the streets and figured that they'd best get out of town, which they did promptly.

Settling In

Although Paul's apartment had been fine for one person, it was a little tight for two. Luckily, a larger space opened up, and with the help of some of his friends, the new couple moved into it. Some new furniture was in order then, as Mouse needed a place for her clothes. The search for an affordable bureau and vanity led to their discovery of auctions and flea markets and by the time they'd end up moving back into the castle, they had quite a bit of moving to do as the couple had become addicted to thrift shopping.

They'd been invited to move back to the castle because "good help" was still so hard to find, and they wanted Mouse back. She knew the ropes. She knew where the emergency ward was. She could cook. Paul could commute to his teaching job, they figured, and she'd be bringing in a better salary than she'd make in a dress shop.

They took over the whole front half of the third floor where Mouse had previously, at one time or another, slept in each of the rooms. The area had probably once been either for the children or guests as it was separated from the back half of the third floor by a door.

They had two turret rooms and a commanding view of the houses down the hill from the leaded glass bathroom windows. You could fill the fabulous old tub as far up as you wanted. The commute from Paul's teaching job was a little longer than it had been, but the proximity to antique and flea markets was a plus and they both enjoyed the hunt.

Mouse, though, would sometimes get to feeling a little antsy during the day and be tempted to look for a little fun from time to time. But she so did not want to destroy her marriage. Still... she strayed a few times, visiting a playmate from college days during the day while Paul was teaching and the kids were all at school. She was doing it because she could not seem to convince herself not to. She couldn't figure out how to stop herself... until she did. Pregnancy. That would do it. That would keep her out of the running. And so would the resulting offspring. She and Paul had talked very specifically about not having children; he'd been an only child and didn't seem keen to share the attention, while she'd simply had enough of that job... but... if it might save their marriage, she was willing to take the chance.

Without saying a word, she went off the birth control pills she'd been taking for quite some time. Within two months, she was pregnant, but she waited to share the information. She didn't want to have to fend off talk of abortion, so she'd tell him when it was too late to even think about it.

Paul was not even a little pleased when he got the news, although his parents, whom Mouse had only met on the weekend of their wedding, were thrilled. Mouse hadn't gotten to know his parents at all, but it was pretty clear from what little time she had spent with them that they weren't all that keen on her, at least his mother wasn't. But they were so keen on the thought of having a grandchild that the next thing she knew, they were dead set on building 'the kids' a house, not in Pennsylvania, but in the tiny town in New Jersey where Paul's father had grown up and where his father's mother still lived, alone, in the house where she'd birthed all her children.

As it happened, the land on which the grandmother's house sat had plenty of available land for building and, at her son's request, she gifted it to Paul so that he and his father and a number of Mouse's brothers could, over the course of the coming summer, build him and his about-to-be family a house. Come summer, the building crew left the castle every morning en masse, returning in time for dinner.

Come summer, Mouse was already surprisingly large, so much so that standard maternity clothes in her size were too small. The larger sizes went around her but fell off her shoulders. She also had trouble finding clothes in pure cotton. She didn't like the feel of synthetics and so determined to make herself a couple of dresses that would both look and feel good, which she set about doing and she was exceptionally pleased with the results. Mouse was used to being ogled and she'd missed that while being so blatantly pregnant and dressed like a shopping bag, so she designed her summer dresses to make the most of her new-found cleavage and got all the attention she could have hoped for. She enjoyed the shock her appearance inspired. She even got a few offers. She was tickled.

A couple of weeks past her due date, Mouse was still running the household and necessary errands. Pregnancy had never slowed her mother down; she had no model for taking it easy. So, when Paul asked her to drive with him out to drop his car off for repairs one October evening, she hopped in the family's VW bus, somewhat hampered by her feet being barely able to reach the pedals because her belly so distanced her from the steering wheel.

The repair shop was not far away, but night had fallen by the time they got there. The "shop" looked a lot more like a shack and was set about half a block off of the main road on a dirt road. She'd never even known it was there and she'd lived in the area for years.

When they'd arrived at the "shop," Paul got out and went inside, asking her to wait just to make sure everything was in order. Not one to waste gas or energy, Mouse turned the car around so that she'd be ready to leave when he gave her the go-ahead. She turned off the engine and relaxed as much as she could, given the circumstances.

Paul finally came out and up to the window to let her know that she could take off. She nodded, turned the key in the ignition and nothing happened. She waited a few moments and tried again. Still nothing.

"You need gas?" hollered a voice from inside.

"No," Mouse shouted back, "got plenty."

She tried again.

Nothing.

The mechanic wandered out to see what was up. "Try the lights."

She did. Nothing happened.

The mechanic pulled something out of his pocket, knocked around the battery and announced, "Your battery's dead. Gonna have to jump-start 'er. You just stay there, and we'll give you a push."

Mouse had jump-started a car many times, but not ten months pregnant, in the dark, on a very steep, very short hill.

"Paul," she said. "No."

"I can't do it," he said, "I don't know how to."

Much swearing commenced inside the vehicle. Then she called out to the owner, who simply turned his back on her and walked back inside. Frustrated and angry, she shouted back at Paul, "Just push it, then, damnit."

He did.

Terrified, she clung to the wheel, intent on keeping it on the narrow rock-spattered, muddy excuse for a road and somehow, she did. Once on the flat area below, she maneuvered the bus around and struggled with it to get back up the hill.

Paul got in. She said nothing. He said nothing. They drove back to the castle in their separate vehicles and went up to their room in heated silence. The next day was moving day.

Emotionally and physically exhausted, Mouse dropped to the bed. Paul followed suit silently after turning on the television. The Bob Newhart show was on, and Mouse was glad for the comic relief... right up until she'd laughed just a little too hard and her water broke.

Paul called the Obstetrician's answering service, received instructions, grabbed the already packed bag, and followed his wife back downstairs to the aforementioned VW bus. It was mid-night when they arrived at the hospital; the staff was ready for her, gave her a once-over, and took her to one of the labor rooms. Labor pains, which she knew about in name only, came as a horrible surprise. She'd had no idea it could hurt that much. Her mother had never mentioned anything like this, but then her mother had never mentioned much about pregnancy, in general, to begin with, despite the fact that it was a state in which she had spent a large percentage of time.

Mouse begged for drugs to numb the pain. One thing her mother *had* told her was that she had been drugged when she'd given birth to Mouse. The nurse refused. "You can do this," she said. "We try to avoid painkillers. They can affect the baby's ability to breathe and, frankly, they don't seem to affect the pain level of mothers all that much." Mouse recalled her mother's narrative regarding her birth and that she'd had to be resuscitated. She determined that if they could resuscitate her in the 1940s, then they could sure as hell resuscitate whatever baby was refusing to leave her body in the 1970s. She continued to beg for relief.

The baby was born hours later, after 10:00 AM, and it hadn't gone easily. As the infant entered the birth canal, a beeper started sounding. What seemed to Mouse like sudden panic ensued and one nurse reported, "No heartbeat!"

As the activity around her picked up, she grew angry. Inside herself, she was screaming, "Die on me? Die on me? After all this? I will fucking kill you myself." Her anger was as visceral as it gets and then... he was out and whisked off to the side somewhere where they re-started him. They wouldn't give him to her just yet but assured her that he was okay and that they would bring him to her once she was settled back in her room.

Paul was updated and went off to notify the grandparents. Mouse was taken to her room, physically and emotionally spent. When she and her baby finally went home, it would be to a home she'd never been in. The move had been scheduled to occur that very day, the truck had been rented, her brother's help had been enlisted, and so, it had happened.

New Things

Mouse had helped Paul design the plans for their house but had not seen the house itself. Everything was there now, as the move had gone on as scheduled. Still somewhat overwhelmed by her own experience, she was, as might be expected, somewhat underwhelmed by the house and somewhat overwhelmed by the reality that she was in her husband's domain now, not hers. His armor and weapons had already claimed all the available wall space. His grandmother lived next door. The folks down the street were cousins. And she had this baby that was their baby, and she couldn't go upstairs and get away from it all because all of it was everywhere.

On the first morning that she awakened in the house, up before Paul or the baby had arisen, she wandered downstairs to stare out the picture window that opened out to show the yard and the woods beyond. Just on the other side of the small creek that ran behind the property, an eerie sight appeared from the low-lying fog that hung above the shallow rivulet below: a mother opossum—entirely white—followed by her babies, four of them, just as ghostly as she, was moving slowly along the bank.

A strange omen, she thought.

Years later, she would learn, in a book called Animal-Speak, that the appearance of the possum was, indeed, a kind of omen as the opossum has a great deal to do with "acting," with playing at something that isn't 'true.' Mouse had been and would be doing a lot of that.

Paul's parents were staying at the grandmother's house, but they'd likely be returning to their Florida home soon. That held the promise of some relief, but the baby… he would be there, 24/7 and he seemed to her like an angel that had somehow embodied, and she knew, with every cell in her body, two things: 1) she, of all people, did not deserve an angel, and 2) she didn't know how to love either angel or baby. She wasn't even sure that she knew what love was. The only person she'd ever felt love from was her father and that love, she recognized but couldn't pinpoint, was somehow not right.

There was a day, months later, when the grandparents had left, and Paul was at school, that she found herself standing at the kitchen window of her house, holding Augustus cradled in her right arm, the morning sun accentuating the golden curls that were growing in, when he caught her eye and seemed to be looking right into her soul, and she shut down. Emotionally, she withdrew from him with the full knowledge that she did not deserve this child and could not give him whatever this was he seemed to be asking of her with his eyes.

Their relationship was never quite the same.

She would stare at him as he slept in his crib, singing, with tears in her eyes that would last as long as she lived, "You are my sunshine, my only sunshine; you make me happy when skies are grey. You'll never know, dear, how much I love you. Please don't take my sunshine away."

She could not give him what he needed and while it broke her heart—and possibly his—she did not know what to do about it. It would be many decades before she was able to release herself from the chains that she didn't even realize had been holding her heart prisoner.

Expanding

Augustus had been born in October, and it would be spring before he and Mouse were ready to explore the neighborhood a bit. Strolling Augie around the neighborhood in his stroller, she would meet the cousins down the street and the great aunt and uncle around the block who kept a wonderful vegetable garden.

It was a challenging year for Paul as a member of the Teacher's Union at the school where he was teaching and it was a challenging year for Mouse as a first-time mother, but they were about as content as could be expected. As Augie grew more active and demanding of her attention, though, Mouse got to wondering if he might not benefit from having a sibling or, perhaps, more correctly, she got to wondering if she might not benefit from his having a sibling. So, all on her own, again, she decided to stop taking birth-control pills.

It didn't take long and, once again, she hid it from Paul until it was too late to do anything about it. This time, though, she determined, it was going to be an entirely different experience. She'd observed that her mother's last pregnancy had been positively celebratory for her. For whatever reason, she had been moved to try "natural childbirth," and not only did she applaud the ease of the delivery, but something also happened for her that had never happened with any of her previous births: she had actually bonded to her child.

There was no handing her new baby off to the help or to her eldest daughter for diaper changes, etc. She didn't take a vacation from work or anything that drastic, but her behavior at home had been so dramatically different that there was an aura of jealousy that had been generated and, as he entered into the independence of childhood, he had to keep an eye out for himself as sibling 'tricks' were not out of the question.

Mouse determined that she would try this natural childbirth thing as she did not want to go through anything like the birth of Augie ever again. She approached Paul and told him that she would like to find classes in natural childbirth, and he told her that she could not. First of all, it would likely cost money. Secondly, he had no intention of being any part of it.

Knowing from experience that "No" meant "No," Mouse headed for the local library and took out a book on the subject. She copied out all the instructions, hid them in her bureau, studied them during the day when Paul was at work, and went over them as she fell asleep at night. She talked to the unborn child in her womb, explaining how things were going to unfold and they began unfolding at a challenging time as Mouse awakened to what she recognized as labor pains on Thanksgiving morning.

Her in-laws, now living in Florida, were spending Thanksgiving and the weekend with "Nanny" in her house on the corner. Her mother-in-law was slated to bring over condiments and dessert. Mouse was responsible for the turkey and the rest of the meal.

This, though, was going to be her baby, her way, so she said nothing about labor pains, going about her business while managing, from time to time, to discretely lean against the nearest piece of large furniture or an appliance in order to breathe through the contractions. She knew that once they were about ten minutes apart, she'd best be on her way to the hospital, which was about half an hour's drive away. No one was going to tell her what to do.

When the contractions had reached about fifteen minutes apart, she realized that she'd probably better speak up as she had not previously factored the likely logistics of a number of surprised people into her equation.

"I'm in labor," she announced as Paul walked into the kitchen. "Take me to the hospital NOW."

Paul stood there as if paralyzed.

"NOW," she repeated, with a tone and timbre she'd never known she had.

Paul held up his index finger as if to say, "Just a second," and dashed out the kitchen door, across the lawn and into his grandmother's house, emerging in less than a minute with his mother not far behind.

Augie wandered in just in time for a quick kiss goodbye.

Mouse felt as pleased with herself as she'd ever felt.

The drive to Philadelphia would be at least a little easier on a holiday morning, but it was still a good half an hour away. Paul was as laser-focused on his task as Mouse was on hers, breathing and holding her breath rhythmically, riding the contractions through. By the time they'd reached the Ben Franklin Bridge, the contractions were a little under two minutes apart. The hospital wasn't far, but he'd have to drop her off at the emergency entrance because there was simply no time to park the car.

When he arrived, staff members approached the car quickly as it wasn't supposed to be there. The entrance was mainly for ambulances, but once Paul had managed to get the words "...less than two minutes..." out of his mouth as Mouse had finally managed to pull herself up and out of the car, they saw the problem and, as if they'd conjured it up out of thin air, there was a gurney at her side and she was being gently maneuvered onto it.

She was passed from attendant to intake nurse to labor nurse to the delivery room with scarcely time to take a breath. The baby practically flew out and Mouse orgasmed as if on cue.

"I've never seen *that* before!" exclaimed the nurse and, almost as an afterthought. "It's a girl."

Mouse turned to see this infant that she had entrusted with a smooth delivery and the moment she saw her, she whipped her head back around toward the delivery nurse and said, "No formula; I'm going to nurse her."

She startled herself. She didn't know where that had come from. Right up until that very moment, she had found nursing to be just this side of disgusting. Why would you if you didn't have to? Her mother had never nursed a child. Annie had and she'd seen it. And it had repulsed her in a very visceral way.

Annie had endured once-monthly sex and produced a child on the third try, for which she was grateful. She had found sex to be repulsive. She had been divorced not long afterward and her husband left the Hare Krishna tribe, leaving Annie and her boy baby to fend for themselves. Mouse had encountered her one day when Annie had returned briefly to the castle, hoping to acquire funds so that she could fly to California, where the main Hare Krishna Temple was located. That's when

Mouse saw nursing in action and had been put off the whole idea. So Mouse had no idea why she'd said what she said to the nurse, but she had, and she knew that she meant it.

Augustus was not overly pleased about the small interloper that returned home with his mother and all the attention that she was getting. He'd had four adults at his beck and call and had been pretty content. Almost immediately, in response to some of his more aggressive displays, the newcomer acquired an additional name: Baby. She was, and would remain for some time, Baby Gwen, accent on "Baby." Baby Gwen had to be treated with gentleness. She was not a pet like the Saint Bernard they had acquired a couple of years before.

Mouse nursing Gwen, though, put him over the edge. He wanted to do that too. Mouse, knowing nothing about child psychology, refused him. She would regret that later after she had joined a local nursing mothers' group that she'd discovered. She needed support because no one in her immediate surroundings was even the least bit supportive of her efforts... except, of course, Baby Gwen, who couldn't seem to get enough of her and who, unlike her older brother, who had been content to sit in a bouncy chair and watch what was going on around him, clung to her mother as if her life depended on her because, from her point of view, it probably felt that way. Mouse wore her in a simple sling-like contraption and went about her household business as usual.

To Paul's extreme discomfiture, Mouse, feeling the need for moral support, discovered the existence of a La Leche League that met once a week in the evening. Children were, of course, welcome, so Paul didn't object. Mouse impressed a visitor to the group who was doing a local news story and she—Mouse—ended up on the local news briefly, addressing the benefits of nursing.

One thing Paul did enjoy was the sight of his wife's newly enhanced breast size… and so did most of the local gas station attendants, lawn maintenance employees, and the workers at the fencing company down the street. Mouse enjoyed the attention and found her mind wandering to places it really shouldn't go. She was grateful for the children's constant presence. This had been her goal, part of her plan to keep her out of trouble, and it was working.

That said, there was something inside her, something she carried on a subconscious level, that drove her to make the most of her newly enhanced breasts and she adjusted her wardrobe accordingly. When summer hit, her standard goin' shoppin' outfit was short shorts, high heels, and a tank top that left nothing to the imagination. She loved the attention… but it was more than that… she loved the desire she felt directed her way. It was as if everything she'd been working to suppress had returned with a vengeance.

The children, at this point, were supposed to be serving as a sort of armed guard, but many of her more ardent admirers were so consumed with her as to hit on her with her children present. But children grow up and they go to school, although by that point, another safeguard—an unwanted one—had entered the picture.

Paul's parents had built a house next door.

Paul's parents had been living in Florida, having moved there for all the reasons that older people do. They'd come up for an extended period to build the house but had, thankfully for Mouse, returned once everything had settled down.

But one day, a dreadful, frightening accident threatened to claim Augustus' life. It had been terrifying for Mouse, who had been alone in the house with her babies. Augustus was just a little over two years old at the time and Mouse had been tending to the laundry in the basement, Gwen was napping. Augustus decided to join his mother and had been descending the open stairway, singing to himself, and was only about a third of the way down when he missed a step and fell—head first—to the cement floor.

Mouse was there so quickly that she barely recalled moving. He was crying. That was good, she figured. He was alive. There wasn't much bleeding, but his skull was obviously crushed. She swept him up and went upstairs to call 911.

A half an hour, they'd said.

A half an hour.

He could be dead by then.

She called the pediatrician's office to inform them of what had happened and that she would be driving him to the hospital. She then lay him down while she ran upstairs to get Baby Gwen, whom she ran to the car, affixing her in the passenger seat. Back to the house for Augie, whom she carried to the backseat of the car, lying him down as carefully as she could. The hospital was normally a thirty-minute ride away; she made it in twenty, praying the whole while that a police car might stop her and get him there faster, but this was a rural area for miles around and that didn't happen.

The doctor's office had called ahead, and they were expecting her at the emergency entrance. Since they had much of the information they needed from the pediatrician's office, they disappeared with him in a flash.

Gwen was asleep. Mouse knew that she had to clear the area, so she located a parking spot where she could cry until she could manage to pull herself together enough to answer questions and give them whatever information they might need.

What felt to her like an eternity passed before anyone could tell her anything. Finally, the pediatrician appeared to let her know that Augie would be alright. There would be a few challenging days ahead, but he felt, in light of the common sense and intelligence she'd shown, that she could handle it at home. He'd have to be assessed about every two hours, day and night, until the swelling subsided, which might take a couple of days. Bandaging, of course, would have to be taken care of as well, but he would be OK. She should call for a follow-up appointment in a week or so, though.

The orderlies helped Mouse back to her car, helped to secure the children and asked her if she felt confident about driving home, which she did. She wasn't unphased by what she'd just been through, but driving to an emergency ward, at this point in her life, was second nature.

Paul got home from school not long after Mouse had arrived. Everything was settled in. Gwen was securely attached to her mother, as per usual, and Augie was napping upstairs. Once Mouse had relayed the events of the afternoon, Paul was beside himself. "But how did this happen... how did it happen? Weren't you watching him?"

Of course, she had been, to the extent that it had seemed necessary. Augie had been walking downstairs, something that he had been doing every day for quite some time... except for the singing part. She was calm in the face of questioning; she knew that she'd done as well as could be expected. And she spent that night and many nights following sleeping at his side, frequently waking to check on him. She trembled just thinking about what had happened.

When her in-laws had called from Florida a few days after the event with their usual "How's everything going?" greeting, Mouse knew that she had to tell them what had happened. But she had no way to expect what was coming.

In less than a week, they had sold their Florida home, moved into his mother's home on the corner, purchased the land between her house and Paul's, and gotten a permit to build. Mouse was despondent, but there was nothing to be done.

Coping

Paul's parents took over her life because, as they saw it, she wasn't fit to run it. Once the house was erected, it was understood that his mother now ran the show... not just her show, everybody's show. Grocery shopping became a group event. Mouse's manner of dress was a daily matter of concern. The overly large dog was banished from the house and a doghouse and small fenced-in area were established. To Mouse's delight, though, her husband brought home, over the course of the next year, two somewhat smaller dogs that were allowed to live inside.

Once the children were old enough for school, it was determined that Mouse should find a job, not that she wanted one. "Gramma" would watch the kids. Pops, which is what the children called their grandfather, had a job at a furniture store that was rumored to have some link to the local mob. What, exactly, he did there was never clear. It was strongly suggested that Mouse apply for a job there as she was sure to get it, so she did and she did.

Oops.

The store was family owned and run. The grandfather, an ancient man, sat in a ratty, uncomfortable-looking armchair just to the side of the office space, by the back door, not far from where Mouse would be working, mostly keeping track of inventory. It was impossible for her not to notice the men who would drop in from time to time to have hushed conversations with him. They looked like thugs but were dressed in obviously expensive suits. The conversations were never long or loud and the men never addressed anyone else in the place.

She also couldn't help but notice that her father-in-law was practically never there. He was always "out on the road," ostensibly repairing appliances.

The man who owned and ran the store was always exquisitely well-dressed and usually well out of sight. His son, however, a young man perhaps ten years or so younger than Mouse and also very well dressed, was in and out and around all the time and he took a keen interest in the new relatively young woman who'd come on board. He'd often ask her to accompany him for a consultation "upstairs" to the second floor, which was, as was the rest of the store most of the time, customer-free. His intentions could not have been more obvious, and Mouse was intrigued. The job was boring as hell and why not?

While she was working there, she also met and became friends with a local hairdresser who had also obviously picked up on the vibe she was generating, and before she knew it, she was entertaining a threesome. That only happened twice, though. Both times she'd felt as if the guys really just wanted to have sex with each other and that she was just a conduit allowing them to feel okay touching each other's penises.

Unfortunately, her father-in-law had also picked up the vibe and suggested that she might like to join him someday to go watch "a woman being fucked by a goat." She was horrified at the thought of both aspects of that offer. First, that bestiality was apparently an available entertainment. Second, her father-in-law was seeking her company for such a taboo outing.

She complained to Paul about it, and he would not believe her. He thought she was just trying to get out of driving to work with him so that she could be on her own.

Not too long afterward, fate stepped in.

She saw it on the news: Playboy was going to open a casino in Atlantic City and a Bunny Hunt would soon be underway. They gave the time, dates, dress requirements, and places where interviews would be held. Mouse had practically been reared on Playboy. It was an integral part of her childhood. She had longed to be a pin-up girl—like the ones Vargas painted—when she grew up. But she was small-breasted and large-waisted and didn't have the body for it. Being a bunny would most likely be the closest she'd ever get to that dream.

She told Paul about the open call and Paul, ignorant of her extra-marital meanderings, probably imagining what a feather in his cap it would be to be married to a Playboy Bunny, told her to go for it.

It was an experience like none other. The interviews were held at a local Marriot. The parking lot was packed, and the lobby was a-swarm with women, most of whom looked to be in their twenties, most of whom were toting clipboards. Mouse quickly and easily found her way to the source of both information and clipboards, signed in, and then found a place to sit and fill out the application, which ranged from the standard "name, age, address" to the less frequently encountered "weight, height, ever been incarcerated" questions.

It was easily twenty minutes before her name was called, but considering the volume of female humanity present, that seemed quick. Her name had been among about eight names that had been called out all at once and the women were then gathered up, herded into an elevator, and transported to a higher floor where another group of women were waiting to descend.

The room they entered felt cramped, though it was, in its normal state of being, a bedroom, probably fairly spacious. But there were no beds here now, only tables and chairs and a series of make-shift dressing rooms where applicants could change into the required heels, pantyhose, and swimsuit, an outfit appropriate for judging someone who would, essentially, be wearing that as a uniform.

The interview was speedy and efficient and not unlike any interview one might have in applying for any job as a waitress anywhere. A couple of Polaroids were taken. Then the entire group was escorted out to meet the next elevator dropping off its bevy of beauties. They'd all be hearing back, one way or another, in the next couple of months, they were told, and the women scattered back to their vehicles and their lives as usual.

Mouse didn't give it too much thought over the passing weeks. It had been an interesting experience, and, after all, she was thirty-five...

The telegram blew her away. She'd been hired. Bunny training would begin in a month.

When she called her father to tell him of her triumph, remembering her childhood days, mesmerized by the Vargas girl cartoons in the magazine he received every month, and the centerfolds, he hit the roof. It was an exceedingly short conversation, and she was stunned. Her mother, on the other hand, was delighted. Mostly, her mother had really liked that it had made her father angry. They'd been divorced for a while now; he'd married a younger woman who bore an exceedingly strong resemblance to Mouse. Polly was glad that Mouse had made him angry because she was still angry with him.

Mouse did not expect the rigorous two-week-long training on how to garnish and then serve cocktails via the Bunny Dip, a presentation she would still reflexively perform whenever delivering drinks for company, even into her seventies. She was taken aback to find that her weight would be monitored daily; it was not to vary from her hire weight by more than a pound either way. Her makeup 'look' was determined for her, and she was taught how to recreate it. Every shift, each bunny had to pass inspection before being let out of the dressing room.

When the Bunny uniform that she had been measured for and then received was a good eight to ten inches smaller in the waist than she was, and the cup size, a good two sizes larger than her own, she became concerned. The woman in the wardrobe assured her, though, that it was perfect and went on to explain how that was so.

Even if your waist was not exceedingly small, it would be by the time you got into your uniform. That was the point of the uniform. It was, essentially, an elaborate corset. It also turned out that all Playboy Bunnies have the same cup size; not for nothin' did they call it a uniform. If you were a bunny, you had C-cup-sized breasts. If your breasts were too small, you propped them up on (very specifically) balled-up pantyhose or men's athletic sweat socks. Both of these items tend to stay put, allowing the breasts to be served up nicely, jiggling ever so slightly, just as they are supposed to. If the breasts were too large, they were squeezed into the boning of the costume, wherever and however they would fit in there. As a rule, in almost all cases, someone else has to zip up one's uniform. It was the first time in her life that Mouse celebrated having smallish breasts.

Pantyhose and their iron-woman-like qualities also came into play as legwear. A bunny was required to wear not just one but two pairs of support pantyhose. "Breasts jiggle; thighs don't," was the motto. Three-inch heels were standard.

At the interview, Mouse had been told that the main requirements for a bunny were a nice smile and great legs. She'd wondered about that at the time, but once she saw how the uniform worked, she understood why: the uniform had been designed to make everything else work the way the company wanted it to. It was about as far from comfortable as one could get, but, as with so many things in her life, she got used to it.

Mouse had always had a natural sway to her walk, which the three-inch heels combined with a constricted waist of the uniform exaggerated and even though her official bunny name was Nikki, pretty much everyone called her Boom-Boom.

The shifts that each woman worked were based on a lottery system, and swaps were allowed on an individual basis. Mouse wanted day work, which most bunnies didn't, preferring the two later shifts as nighttime was where the really big tipping usually happened and the tipping was necessary because the hourly wage was as minimal as it could get. She got her to wish for day work with no trouble.

She learned to love people while she was working the day shift at Playboy. She learned that most people—at least most of the older people that she spoke with—had enjoyed rich and interesting personal lives. They showed her pictures of their families, they shared their stories, and she felt honored that they wanted to. It was an experience such as she had never had. The buses that came in every day generally brought older people who played the slot machines, and, unlike the players at the tables, who were usually dead serious about their games and the money they won, the older folks who played the slot machines acted as though they were on holiday, just having a good time. It was at Playboy that she met her first actual bearded lady who had been taking a break from the circus for the day.

Perhaps the best thing about training for Mouse had been the opportunity to meet other bunnies with whom she could carpool. Since Atlantic City was a good hour away from home, it was great to have company. After training, though, because the hours were from morning well into the night and broken up into shifts, it was back to solitary drives, which, for Mouse, anyway, provided other benefits, some of which ended up giving her venereal warts. It wasn't that she couldn't say no, it was that she didn't seem to want to and would go out of her way to put herself in positions of, sometimes, downright danger... and she knew it.

Oddly, her main concern was not being killed but making sure that the police would have enough information to find the perpetrator. If she'd made arrangements to meet someone in an abandoned ice cream joint a little way down the boardwalk, she'd always make sure to pull one of the other bunnies out of the bar and point out the man she planned to leave with.

"If I don't show up for work tomorrow," she'd tell her. "That's the guy you tell the police to look for."

Needless to say, it's difficult to keep venereal diseases secret from the man you're sleeping with. Paul was generous in going along with the pretense that this was all just random, so it didn't stop.

On another front, something unusual came up one night at home when Paul had some friends from school over. They were having drinks and smoking marijuana in the room at the back of the house while Mouse was sitting with the kids, watching television in the TV room. Mouse always had, for whatever reason generally eschewed smoking, drugs and alcohol. One of the guests, feeling sorry for her because she could not join them—not that she wanted to—bought her a brownie that one of the visitors had made. Mouse thanked him, didn't give it a second thought, and munched on the brownie as she watched TV. Slowly, she began to feel very strange. Then she realized what had happened: the brownie had been laced with marijuana! She panicked. She'd ingested drugs. She didn't know what to do; she couldn't undo it! So, she did what she always did when she was in trouble; she called her father.

She told him what had happened.

There was dead silence on the other end of the line.

Then he spoke, "I'm ashamed of you," in a tone as serious as she'd ever heard from him.

Her heart seemed to fall in her chest. He'd never before chastised her.

And then, as gently as if he were talking to a child, he followed up, saying, in a soft, slow tone of voice, "You know what to do… just… relax."

As if hypnotized, Mouse simply hung up the phone without saying or hearing another word. She walked to the stairs, walked up the stairs, went into her daughter's bedroom, lay down on the bed, and closed her eyes.

She had no idea how long she'd been there when Paul came in sounding vexed. "What are you doing?" he queried, his voice colored by a mixture of anger and confusion.

"Oh!" she said, feeling as if she were in a trance, rolling over sideways to look at him. "I don't know," she replied, groggy but honestly. It would be decades before she realized that she had just been following the programming she'd once received as a child.

It was not long after that that Mouse made the decision to leave her husband and her family and move in with one of the Bunnies on her shift. Her behavior, she recognized, was not conducive to being a part of a family. The young woman's parents had turned their shore house over to their daughter and she had been looking for a renter to help cut costs. Giving Paul very little reason or time and leaving him to explain to the children, she left home. She made arrangements to pick up Gwen and Augie every other weekend, giving her every *other* weekend to go where she wanted and do as she pleased.

By now, there was an older man who ran a hair salon that she had been seeing on the sly, as well as an exceedingly handsome man from Pennsylvania who came to the club to gamble once a week in the afternoons. Her new free time gave her the opportunity to explore those relationships.

The older gentleman, Mel, lived up the coast and once she was freed of her domestic obligations, he invited her up for a weekend, during which extended time together, she discovered that he was a user of cocaine and that his sexual proclivities were both very odd and way outside of her comfort zone. That was the end of that. The younger man, however, was both an absolute gentleman and a guy who liked to have conversations. He was intelligent. He was also married, but he often took her out to dinner, and they had a great time together. She also hung out more with the dealers from the tables whom she'd never really gotten to know as a waitress. It was one of them who got her, for the first time in her life, drunk. The evening did not turn out as he'd imagined it might and she never drank another alcoholic beverage, save the infrequent glass of wine just to be polite.

She also received a fascinating proposition from an adorable older gentleman who held a high-level position with a well-known cosmetics company. Her bunny friend, Fancy, had a friend like that who put her up in a fabulous condo, gave her a remarkable allowance, and all she had to do was be available to him on weekends that he was in town. Mouse received a similar offer from her adorable friend: $5,000 a month and a condo on the condition that if he was in town, she'd be all his.

She couldn't bring herself to do it. She only had the weekends to see her children and she could not compromise that. She'd done enough harm to them already.

The weekend that she'd received that offer, she returned to the house she'd been staying in with a bunny friend to discover. While Mouse had been gone, her friend had returned home one day to discover a young man hidden in the house. He had restrained her and raped her, threatening her at knifepoint to ensure her compliance. She'd already been to the police by the time Mouse arrived, but she was still devastated. The process of viewing a line-up and having to provide a sketch artist with details of his face had only added to her anxiety.

Mouse felt terrible. She felt guilty for not having been there, but her friend said that the young man described to her how he'd been watching the house for quite some time and that it was her, specifically, that he was after. He'd had it all planned out. There was no way it wasn't going to happen at some point as far as he'd been concerned.

Health Issues

The pain that Mouse had been experiencing in her mid-section for a few weeks seemed to be increasing in intensity. She'd chalked it up to nerves, what with everything that had been going on, but it was getting impossible to ignore. She made an appointment to see her doctor in Philadelphia because she'd been seeing him since she had been in her teens; he'd delivered her children. The diagnosis was not as bad as the pain had felt it might be: uterine cysts. "But you'll want them removed before they get worse," he'd cautioned. A date was set for surgery, and two weeks off from work were noted. The surgery went off without a hitch... sort of.

When the doctor came into her room post-op to go over the surgery, he said, "Oh, and I did your husband a favor while I was there and tightened things up a little."

Still a bit woozy, Mouse had no outward response to that. Her mind, however, was disconcerted. *What did he do? What exactly did he do?*

Since recovery time was around three months, it would be a while before she discovered the truth of the matter and how much, exactly, intercourse would now be more a matter of pain management for her than anything else.

Mouse began to wonder about this life she'd chosen. It seemed as if it was becoming exponentially more disturbing. The next time she went to pick up the children, she mentioned casually to Paul that she thought that she might have been making some pretty poor choices. Since that was perhaps the deepest understatement that Paul had ever heard, he simply nodded knowingly.

When she brought the children home again, he met her at the door and asked her if she'd be willing to consider going to counseling and she said that she would. He asked if he could come to visit her at the shore the following weekend and she agreed.

Laying Foundations

The next weekend Paul showed up with flowers. They walked the beach and talked. They lay on a blanket on the beach and talked. He'd found a counselor, he said, but she wasn't feeling quite ready to move home yet. After all, there was more to deal with than just Paul and her babies, who were hardly babies anymore… there were the in-laws. There was the whole prospect of the job she'd left at the furniture store to which they—the in-laws—might want her to return. After all, they knew that they knew how to raise a child and she didn't.

Finally, Mouse agreed.

A week or so later, Mouse and Paul met at the office of the counselor he had found. To her surprise, it was a woman. She felt comfortable with that. Questions and answers were exchanged all around and a sort of format was established for the visits.

Paul was anxious for Mouse to return home, but Mouse wanted to feel as if they could establish some sort of a format, with the help of the counselor, of what was expected, given the dynamic of living next door to two people who had no idea of how to mind their own business. That could take a couple of visits. Also, the counselor had asked to see each of them separately as well as together.

Mouse very much enjoyed her private visits as she could talk more openly about her "adventures." The counselor was so impressed... or stunned... or overwhelmed... by Mouse's confessions that she finally said to her, "You know, you could write these experiences down and probably get paid for them."

Mouse took her words with a grain of salt, but before she left, the woman asked her to please write one of her experiences up as a story. "You may find it helpful," she said. "Just try it... and bring it in next time you come."

What the heck, Mouse thought to herself, *couldn't hurt.*

On her return visit, she bought the completed piece along and left it with the counselor. On the following visit, the counselor spent more time talking about her potential as a writer of erotic fiction than about the dynamics of her marriage. But she'd already made the needed impact on both Paul and Mouse and soon they were getting down to the crux of what seemed to be the root cause of Mouse's dissatisfaction and discomfort and Paul was hearing what she was saying. What she was saying was that the presence of his parents in almost every aspect of their life was driving her crazy. That it was as if his mother, specifically, felt that somehow, she was supposed to be running the show.

As life would have it, not long after their conversation, Mouse received a call from her mother saying that she was planning to leave the Philadelphia area and move to Miami. She'd received an excellent offer from a pediatric hospital there and it didn't hurt that her former husband was living in the area. Despite his reprehensible behavior, she still loved him.

The hospital wanted her as soon as possible, though, and she had to sell the house. It was perfect timing. Mouse and Paul could move in with the kids while the house was on the market, Paul's parents would still be within driving distance, but at least they wouldn't be on the back steps. Both were eager to get their marriage back on track, so they determined to go for it.

On her next visit to the counselor—Paul had decided that he was "fine" and didn't need any more counseling, so she was alone—the counselor strongly suggested that she submit her work to one of the more prestigious men's magazines. "If nothing else," she'd said, "it'll be a little extra income."

As for the move to her mother's home in Wyncote, there was nothing to stand in their way. The move was expeditious and before she knew it, they were settling in, just in time to get Augie and Gwen registered for the elementary school, which was only about four blocks away. The house itself was directly across the street from the high school, which seemed to be one of the reasons that it hadn't sold yet. For them, it was perfect.

The house came with an occupant as well, one of Mouse's younger brothers, who'd gone to college in the area and was working for a large corporation nearby. It was the kind of job he was made for, and it paid really well. So, there was a built-in babysitter who was as playful as a child himself but also brilliant... homework help was readily available.

Mouse was delighted to find out that there were adult night courses at the school across the street and that one of the courses was Dance. There was still nothing in the world that Mouse loved to do as much as she loved to dance and there hadn't been much of that available to her for a long, long time, not since she'd been a go-go girl at the college dances. She signed up.

The instructor was a former professional dancer, Hedy Tower, then in her 80s, who moved with the lithe, graceful strength of a well-trained 20-year-old. The class consisted mostly of women, but there were a few men as well, one of whom caught Mouse's eye at just about the same time that she'd caught his, but the class was about to start.

Class started with what Hedy called "stretching." Mouse cherished the class and loved going, but it was the stretches that her body responded to most strongly. Well, that and the good-looking Italian guy. She liked the stretching so much that she began stretching every morning after she dropped the kids at school. She never missed it.

One day, while waiting in an office for an eye exam, she was leafing through one of the well-worn magazines and came across an article on yoga... she had brief flashbacks to her childhood fascination and the old man in the diaper-looking wrap. Then she saw the illustrations... they were the stretches that Hedy had been teaching! She was thrilled. She was doing yoga. One day maybe she'd be as lithe and limber as the old man she'd seen in the encyclopedia! She would continue to do those stretches, as well as a number of others, every day for the rest of her life; even when she was physically unable to move for a while, she would do them in her mind's eye. It was as if, in some way, she could not properly interpret, through yoga, her life was completing itself... like the ouroboros, the snake shown eating its own tail... a symbol of assimilation and rebirth.

So, on the one hand, some aspect of her was taking steps in a new direction, while on the other, well... there was that handsome guy from dance class. It didn't amount to much, but it happened for a while and then just faded away, though not long after, as if fate could not yet release its grasp on her, one day as Paul was driving the whole family back from a shopping spree—the man loved his clothes—and Mouse was sitting in the passenger seat, they were stopped at a traffic light. Mouse looked to her right, just scanning the area and there, directly beside her, sitting in the driver's seat of a very nice Jaguar, was Mr. Nice Guy, the man who used to wine and dine her when she was working in Atlantic City. Her heart went into high gear when he turned, and their eyes met.

What the hell?

If anything had ever seemed fated to be, she figured, that certainly was.

He knew her name. It must have taken no effort whatsoever to get the phone number and first thing Monday morning, just after everyone was off to school, the phone rang. He lived not even ten minutes away from her but, of course, going to either of their homes would be unthinkable, so they determined to meet at a local park that was heavily wooded and for the most part, used only on weekends by the local community.

They continued to meet two or three times a week for months. It was daylight and they were in a public place, so they were limited in their sexual engagement, but because they were conversationally compatible and had always been genuinely interested in each other's lives, they always had plenty to talk about. She was more comfortable with him than she had ever been with anyone.

Meanwhile, back at home, she'd purchased her first typewriter, an IBM Selectric, and had produced her first finished attempt at a professional erotic story which she sent off to Penthouse magazine, not really expecting much from her effort. She had enjoyed the process of writing it, though and figured that the counselor might have been onto something, that this might be an outlet for her energy.

Of course, there was more energy to be dealt with, so she wrote, and she wrote and she wrote and she finally figured out that she'd have to do some research and figure out where else she could send this overflow of energy. She perused the local newsstands and the magazine racks in drugstores and found a few leads, one of them, curiously, was located not far from her. It wasn't very flashy, more like a newspaper than a magazine, with reviews of local massage parlors in addition to a fictional piece or two, but it was a possibility, so she submitted a piece to them and fairly quickly received an enthusiastic response from the editor along with an invitation to meet for lunch at the mall.

His name was Bob. He was tall and lanky and okay looking, but beyond that, his looks did not impress her. He was enthusiastic about her writing, though, and explained to her that their reporters—all two of them— would visit the local "houses," which Mouse immediately understood was short for "houses of prostitution," and then write reviews about their experiences there which were supposed to be actual reviews but were often pure fiction and the "reporters" were far less than skilled in the literary arts. The paper's real purpose was simple: bring in money for advertising from the houses so that they could bring in money to pay the staff.

Bob liked her writing and asked her if she'd like a job as an editor on the paper. She thought she might. *Heaven knows*, she'd thought to herself, *they could use one*. His title was Editor, and he was more *managing* editor than a proofreader, which was what they most definitely needed. She said that she'd run it past her husband and get back to him. Her schedule was flexible, so she managed to drop off the children, be there when they got home, and still find some time for Mr. Nice Guy and so she was in.

And Penthouse published her work, so her ego was stoked as well.

The only thing in her life that wasn't quite working was her relationship with Paul. They'd been married—albeit occasionally living separately—for almost fourteen years, but Mouse and he had never really been on the same page sexually. Mouse may or may not have actually enjoyed sex. It was, without a doubt, something she seemed to require, but it also seemed that it was never enough somehow. She thoroughly enjoyed writing about it, but the actuality of it didn't live up to its hype. It was as if it were similar to an addiction; she craved it, seemingly couldn't get enough of it, yet it was never satisfying. She'd read—and written—a lot about "climax" but wasn't even sure she'd ever had one... until Bob.

And that was all it took, sadly for everyone else in her life, especially her children.

She'd spoken, since the counselor had come into their lives, with Paul directly about her dissatisfaction with their sexual interactions. The fact was that he simply didn't take her into account. He didn't take her desire to be made love to without having her dress up in costumes seriously and when she'd express a desire to try something new or different, he'd blow it off as kinky. She knew—or imagined that she knew—that because Bob had shown her what he could do for her, he would be more open.

Thinking only of her own needs and desires, she confronted Paul and told him that she was leaving and was taking the children with her. His response was that he would never grant her a divorce unless she relinquished the children and that if she did leave and take them, he would, when they were old enough to understand it, tell them the kind of woman that she was.

She balked at that, feeling because of her own guilt and knowing that Paul's mother would be in on the shaming too, that it would all likely be overwhelming for the children and that they would hate her for it... she wasn't all too fond of herself by that time.

So it was that the next day she stood in the upstairs window, watching Paul leading her children away, children he'd never wanted, just to spite her. Augie alone turned back and looked up at her in the window as she dissolved in tears. The look on his face was one she would never forget and it would, every time she recalled it, bring tears to her eyes. Little Gwen, holding her father's hand, probably feeling as secure as she ever had, always trusting, looked straight ahead.

Reality Kicks In

When Paul and Mouse had originally moved into the house, it had come with a special treat for Mouse and the kids, as her brother, Rick, wanted to continue living there. He'd taken an excellent, high-paying job only a short drive away. He loved kids and so when he was home, he and Augie and Gwen had a blast. Rick was sad to see them go as well, but he got along fine with Bob and didn't seem to hold anything against him, so they were happy when he told them, when they asked, that he'd love to stay and they all had a great time together after work, playing board games as a rule. On the weekends, he and Bob played hacky-sack and finally even got Mouse, who had never been much at sports, to play.

Paul had left the dogs behind, an Irish Setter and a Bloodhound, both of whom had been devoted to Mouse, who loved to run with them but the Setter, Mac, developed an allergy to fleas not long after the rest of his family disappeared, and the vets were unable to treat him. He was, essentially, chewing himself up. There was no hope for him, and Mouse finally returned to the vet they'd been seeing, and Mac was euthanized. Two weeks later, someone broke into the fenced-in backyard and stole the bloodhound. Her children were gone and her old friends, the dogs, were gone. She loved her brother dearly and his presence was reassuring, but did she love Bob? *No,* she realized, *not really.* But then she hadn't loved Paul either... if she even knew what that kind of love was. She'd never loved any man except for her father... and that was different... or so she thought, having thoroughly repressed any memory of the years of incest that had taken place.

The house, which had been on the market since before they'd even moved in, finally sold. Rick took advantage of the situation to go house hunting. He was making good money and ready to invest in something. A house seemed like a good idea. He'd never be able to—and really didn't want to—invest in anything as grand as his mother's house was. It had, after all, been housing numerous siblings prior to Polly's move to Florida.

Thus the house hunt began. It went on for a bit. He finally settled on a townhouse in a place called Collegeville that was just far enough outside of the city to feel away from his work but still within easy range of shopping and entertainment. He would have the master bedroom and bath, which were half a flight of stairs up, on the first landing, while Mouse and Bob would have a smaller space on the next landing up. They liked their space as it was at the back of the house and quiet.

Mouse had been, in her spare time, dabbling in art again and the basement of the townhouse offered plenty of un-precious space where she could set up a makeshift studio. She began searching, as well, for other writing opportunities and managed to stimulate some interest at a Philadelphia-based arts newspaper. She began reviewing shows for them.

Bob, however, was disturbed by her explorations. They didn't 'need' that, he claimed, they were doing just fine. But Mouse wanted to expand. She wanted to be doing something… nice. It was that simple. "Well," he countered. "Then they'd do it together." Mouse didn't want to be together. She wanted something that was all her own. She didn't want to run off and have adventures as she once did... she just wanted something she could be recognized for. She wanted acknowledgment.

Bob made the case that they were "One" now and that it was *they* who should be recognized. They should be "Mouse & Bob." He was relentless, ultimately setting up a very large table in the basement studio where they could create something "big."

He then began attending the art shows with her and 'editing' the reviews, ensuring that they all carried the by-line "Mouse & Bob." Her name would always come first, he assured her. She didn't care and she wasn't happy... but it did seem to capture people's interest, so she gave up resisting and before long, people in the local art world knew who Mouse & Bob were.

Mouse had made herself content with what was, but then something happened inside her. It had begun with some digestive difficulties and a little pain in her belly. Slowly, over months, she became more and more uncomfortable. They had no insurance and Mouse, having grown up with pathologists as parents, was leery of medical doctors. Her father had once told her that he'd seen more people in the morgue from "physician error" than from anything else. She researched the local telephone directory and alternative sources, searching for something that "felt right," finally settling on a local nutritionist.

The visit to the local nutritionist turned out to be a not-so-local drive out into the countryside. The local nutritionist herself was drop-dead gorgeous and dressed to kill. Bob found it impossible to refrain from ogling her. Mouse quietly seethed. The nutritionist played her role calmly and thoroughly and, after paying a fee that was a bit surprising, they took the list of supplements she'd recommended to a health food store nearer to home and, again, spent more money than they'd imagined possible to spend in a vitamin shop.

Once home, Mouse read every label and made a chart of when to take what and when. From that point on, the day unfolded like any other day. One of the pills, though, something called ox bile, was to be taken later in the day and she'd neglected to do so around dinner time and figured that she'd take it before she went up to bed. She did. But midway up the last half-flight, she passed out cold on the stairs, which was where Bob found her.

He gathered her up, took her to their bed, and lay her down while he pulled back the sheet on the other side. He then rolled her over to that side. She was awake but limp and seemingly unable to move on her own.

She awoke late the next morning, a Saturday; Bob was already up and elsewhere. As she began to come up out of sleep, she opened her eyes and was astounded that she could see from one side of the room to the other in perfect focus without moving her head.

She closed her eyes and rubbed them. She opened them again. It was the same. She closed her eyes. She couldn't believe it. She opened them again and it was the same: a 180-degree view of the room.

She thought she'd get up but discovered that she was too weak to do it, so she just surrendered, lay back down and continued being amazed by her newfound ability.

Eventually, Bob returned, wondering why she wasn't up yet, and she told him what was going on, also that she didn't seem to be able to get up. This was particularly worrisome to her as they were supposed to have Augie and Gwen with them that weekend. Paul was to drop them off late that afternoon and then they'd return them on Sunday. She determined to call the nutritionist to see what could have gone wrong.

The nutritionist found what Mouse was saying unbelievable, which made Mouse angry as she was mildly terrified. She did not have a regular doctor but felt that she needed to see someone and ended up at a trailer, a traveling medical-assistance vehicle, that made stops throughout the nearby countryside. The folks at the trailer were much nicer than the woman who would henceforth be referred to as The Killer Nutritionist. They listened respectfully, took some sort of X-Ray-like picture, and then wrapped her chest in a very warm, comfortable something and had her lie on a table for a while.

After reviewing the picture they'd taken, they said that they couldn't see anything, prescribed hot packs and rest, and wished her the best of luck. As someone who'd grown up in and around doctors and hospitals, she found it interesting to experience these so-called alternative approaches. She didn't not like it, but, perhaps, needless to say, they did nothing.

When her children showed up that afternoon, they were surprised to find their usually busy-as-a-bee mother bundled up on the couch, which was where she pretty much stayed all day. They watched a lot of TV together; Bob got them dinner, and on Sunday, he helped her out to the passenger seat of the car so that he could drive them home.

Moving

Meanwhile, Brother Rick had received a tip from a neighbor on the house—an actual, free-standing house—that had gone up for sale in nearby Phoenixville. He liked what he saw and entered into the process of making it his.

Moving day found Mouse wrapped in a blanket, curled up on a mattress, as the townhouse was emptied out around her. She felt useless, deeply distressed that she could not help... but she couldn't. She barely had the strength it took to move herself from one place to another.

At the end of the day, when everything except for the mattress she'd been curled up on had been moved to its new location, Bob bundled her up—because she was almost always cold—and took her to what would be their new residence, a small, simple house on a corner lot across the street from a kids baseball field. It had a very small backyard, about a third of which was a plain cement 'patio,' a place where Mouse would, in nice weather, be spending a lot of time resting.

If there was one thing Mouse was good at, it was surrendering. That said, before long, she was in a tremendous amount of pain everywhere... it wasn't just "aching;" it was outright pain. Bob dutifully carted her to doctor after doctor, every one of whom gave her some version of the "You're just getting old" speech. She was livid. She was, after all, only in her 40's and her mother, now in her late 60's, was as spry as ever.

"I've seen 'getting old,' she'd verbally lash back, "I've seen what it is to be tired and worn down. What I'm feeling isn't that! Something is wrong." Her mother, who was footing the bill for all these doctor visits, agreed. She was concerned. She urged Mouse to keep trying. Thanks to Rick's new work schedule, working nights at a print shop, she was able to do that. He slept till sometime after noon, as a rule, but that left him the rest of the afternoon to take her wherever she needed to go.

Finally, it happened: a doctor recognized what was happening to Mouse. He'd noticed something that all the other doctors had either overlooked or just assumed was "age-related." He saw that Mouse was holding her fingers strangely and did not assume, as the previous doctors might have, that it was "just arthritis." He told her that he would like to palpate her hands. That was fine with her.

But the look on his face when he looked up from her hands and told her that what she was suffering from was something called diffuse progressive systemic sclerosis—known more commonly as scleroderma—which meant "hard skin," told her that whatever this scleroderma was that he was telling her about was not good. There was a medication, he told her, that he could prescribe for her that might ease her pain, but it came with side effects, and, no, unfortunately, there was no cure for the disease. She would continue to get harder and harder... eventually inside as well. There was no stopping it.

Mouse sat there for a bit in silence, processing what she'd just been told: she was going to turn into a stone and die.

When she returned to a more mentally accessible state, he asked her to come into his office, where he sat down behind his desk across from her and let her know that he knew that this was a lot to process that, when she was ready, he'd like to schedule some tests on her lungs which seemed to be affected.

Mouse told him that she'd have to consult with her mother as it was her mother who had been covering all these costs. When she mentioned that her mother was a pathologist, he asked if she was from "around there," and Mouse gave him a brief summary of her background and before she'd gotten very far, he blurted out, "She was my teacher!"

If she'd ever had any doubts about this doctor, they'd all just been dispelled. Her mother did not suffer fools lightly and the tone of his voice, coupled with the look on his face, told his story. Somehow, hearing that she had a fatal, incurable disease—perhaps because the news had come from this particular person—was a whole lot easier to take than hearing that she "was just getting old" had been from the dismissive dolts she'd seen before.

Mouse felt better about feeling bad, about being so tired all the time, about not being able to help with the house or play hacky-sack after dinner. It had been her nature to be busy, to do things, or make things, but her body was begging for her to dial all that back, so during the day, when she was mostly alone, she took to reading books and watching old movies on TV.

One morning, having fallen asleep considering possible ways that she might be able to commit suicide that would for sure work, she awoke with a vision. What she saw were seven trees with springtime green leaves growing on a lightly sloping grass-covered hillside. Above them, backed by a brilliant blue sky, were the words—in red—"Seven reasons to live."

She didn't take it lightly, as dreams had always played an important part in her life; they were often as much a part of her life as her waking moments. So, she got out of bed and, still in pajamas, went immediately to paint the image on a small piece of watercolor paper. Later, she would have it framed.

She also began to take walks around the local area, not what you would call 'brisk' walks, just walks. She felt instinctively that her body needed some sort of gentle exercise and since she had lost most of her flexibility, walking seemed like a simple way to fill the bill. She couldn't go far; she didn't have the energy, so she stayed mostly within about a five-block radius of the house. She looked odd and she knew that she looked odd. Her skin had a strange grey quality and her hands had become more like claws.

She didn't want people to feel bad about staring at her and she really didn't like the fact that some small children were actually afraid of her, so she decided, especially for the children's sake, her hands being right about their eye level, to invent something that would give people "permission" to stare at her. With Bob's help, she haunted the local thrift shops till she found a pair of the old-fashioned white gloves that girls had once been required to wear to church and on special occasions. She lopped off the fingers of the gloves as they were of no use to her. They'd never make it around the tightly curled "U"-shapes that all her fingers had become. She then stuffed the 'bodies' of the gloves with rags to get a smooth, firm surface and painted them with symbols and shapes in brilliant colors. This would give children a perfect reason to stare at her without getting in trouble with their parents for staring at "the poor crippled lady." This, by extension, would give their parents a reason to perhaps initiate a conversation.

The results were even better than she'd expected, and she'd often find herself, especially in lines at the grocery store, explaining scleroderma to people or they'd open up to her about some relative of theirs who had it or had died from it.

Also unexpected was the one day, on her walk, when she heard a song playing in her mind… a song she'd never heard before, a song with a very simple tune but which, she imagined, her sub-conscious might have dished up to give her something pleasant to focus on while she was trodding the same streets day after day.

The song even gave itself a name: The Star-Shaped Song

Don't turn around, looking out of doors;
The love you seek, the love that won't un-do;
The love that is your mother and the love you grant the other
Is the Universal Love designed as you.

Love is birth and love is death.

You breathe love with every breath.

Love will BE you, all you need to do is LOVE.

Another Path to Walk

One day, when she'd been watching old movies in the afternoon, between advertisements, a public service announcement came on announcing the formation of a support group for people in chronic pain. The hospital where it was going to be held was about half an hour away from the house. She'd never been a person to join groups of any sort, but this sounded as if it might be useful, so she took down the number, called, and expressed her interest in joining. The woman who had answered the phone was the person who had conceived of the group and was interested in talking with her about why she wanted to join. Eventually, they met in person and ultimately, Mouse attended the official announcement ceremony in the hospital auditorium at which the Board of Directors that she had assembled introduced themselves and spoke a little about the importance and need for such a group.

Each of the members of the audience that had been pre-screened as prospective members of the group was invited to introduce themselves as well. After the meeting was dismissed, one of the physicians from the board hailed Mouse over to where he sat. He told her that he had a friend, a physician, at the Hospital of the University of Pennsylvania, who was currently running a clinical trial that was investigating a possible cure for scleroderma. He told her that he thought that she might have a chance to be a part of it, gave her his phone number, and told her to call in the morning and his secretary would give her all the information she'd need.

Despite having a frustrating time getting home as she realized that she was low on gas and had to fill the tank—something Bob usually did—then found that she was unable to open the cap and had to have assistance with that, she was in a mildly optimistic state of mind, looking forward to a possible adventure.

Tomorrow came, she called the office and got the information she'd been promised. She then called the number she'd been given and discovered that the doctor who'd spoken to her the night before had already called them to alert them to her call. She felt special. She wondered, *though, why? What was it that had earned their attention?*

An appointment was made for the following week for an interview. That, too, seemed curious. That said, the last clinical trial she'd been in had been when she was six months old, so what would she know about protocol?

The interview, as it turned out, had been absolutely necessary because the treatment had a kind of hidden glitch... folks who had decided, after having experienced the treatment, that they no longer wanted to be a part of the trial and had stopped the treatments would die very shortly after missing what would have been their next treatment. That fact was the reason why they were on the lookout for new participants.

Death sounded pretty good to Mouse. She was tired of suffering and told the doctor that potential death didn't sound all that bad. He then let her know that she could not be a part of the trial if she had been taking any drugs that were designed to mitigate the pain. She hadn't! She was so glad that she had turned down the offer of them.

All that was left, then, was to establish her baseline with what was called "the pinch test," take some blood samples and photographs, and she was in. The treatment itself took two days and would require an overnight stay in the hospital. The pinch test and the photos were scheduled for the following week. Mouse was excited. Maybe she'd get better; maybe she'd die. Either way, she figured, it was a win-win situation.

Treatment

Mouse's pinch test was scheduled for the following week, and it was a lot more painful than she'd imagined it might be since her skin was as tight as a drum over almost all of her body and tighter in some places. The final result of her first pinch test was listed as "80% hidebound." She was not thrilled to discover that after every treatment, before returning home, she would have to undergo the pinch test, but it wasn't the worst thing in the world and it might be worth the effort.

Because she lived so far from the hospital, her friend Suzanne, who had been her friend ever since that private school that she'd gone to as a kid, had a townhouse in the city that was perhaps ten minutes from the hospital. For her first treatment, they decided that she should spend the night there. Mouse was nervous and had difficulty falling asleep, so she made sketches of the street outside the window until she couldn't keep her eyes open. Come morning, she was well enough rested to spend most of the day on her back in a bed.

Once she'd parked her car in the covered lot at the hospital, Mouse found her way, with some assistance, to the wing of the hospital where the clinical trial was taking place. She introduced herself at the desk and was booked, then guided to a room where two or three nurses took her temperature, measured her blood pressure, weighed her, and provided her with a blue paper gown that she was unable to tie at the back because her hands, by now, were more like paws, the tips of her fingers were almost resting on the palms of her hands.

Not long after they'd gotten her all tucked into the hospital bed and she was resting back comfortably at an angle, more sitting than not, two nurses—a very pretty white woman with light brown hair and a very jolly-looking black man about twice her weight—came in. His name was Bill, and he was pushing, ahead of him, a metal and glass white box on wheels, which they referred to as UVAR.

Bill explained, in terms that Mouse could understand, what UVAR would do. He and the pretty woman with him would, he explained, be putting a large gauge needle into her arm because they needed to have whole blood cells. That needle would be connected to a tube that led to UVAR's front window-like panel, where it wound from one side to the other in a series of tight U-turns, and for a period of time—three hours or so—her blood would be making round-trips through the tubes being exposed, as it did so, to the ultra-violet light (UV) that UVAR was beaming.

After all the blood had been properly exposed, it would then be returned to her body, but she would be hooked up to the machine the entire time as the blood cycled in and out. Afterward, she'd be on her own and could, for instance, go out for dinner, though she had to spend the night in her room there at the hospital. She'd take advantage of that time, over the many months she was involved with the trial, by making dates with her friends that still lived in Philly, like Suzanne, and her friend from college, Steven.

The ability to have some fun in the midst of two procedures was a genuine treat because while the treatment itself—the blood going out and in and so on—was a very neutral procedure, getting the needle in was most definitely not. Her skin was like leather, not super-soft glove leather, more like saddlebag leather. That alone, on the days of her first two treatments, had been enough to make her consider, on the trip home, if this was really worth it. No one had been cured by the treatment so far. The only upside was that people who had given up on it had died very soon afterward and death seemed almost welcome at this point. Even then... the pinch test had been torturous, but that needle... sigh. She was on the fence.

She got off the fence the next day.

The needle site had been thoroughly bandaged to keep it from bleeding. They'd told her at the hospital that she could switch over to a less bulky bandage by morning. When she did, what she found under the bandage changed everything: the skin, for about half an inch around the point of penetration, was not just soft, it was as soft as the skin of the newborn.

Her whole body relaxed. It would be worth it, the pain... then she realized... there wouldn't be as much pain! It would hurt, sure, but it wouldn't feel like torture.

Once monthly trips to the hospital became no more than a routine happening, usually including dinner with friends. She was starting to feel as normal as she'd ever felt. Her friend, Suzanne, had introduced her to a woman she knew, Ellen, who was a Gestalt therapist and a massage therapist as well. Suzanne gifted Mouse with a session from Ellen that had fascinating ramifications for Mouse.

On her first visit, Ellen taught Mouse how to breathe into her belly. That, she said, would help with the pain. She asked Mouse if she was familiar with statues of Buddha; Mouse was. Ellen told her that the reason Buddha had such a big belly and was always seen smiling was that he was happy and that he was happy because he breathed into his belly. "It relaxes you," she'd told her. Mouse began practicing that day and belly-breathing eventually became the way that she always breathed and would breathe for the rest of her life.

The massage felt good. But at one point, as Ellen worked the muscles on her lower back, she found and 'described' with her fingers for Mouse, a spot that she said she only ever encountered in cases of incest.

"No," Mouse responded neutrally, without a trace of emotion. "That never happened to me. I'd remember."

Ellen responded with a heavy sigh and continued her work. Ellen had been right, of course, but it would be another couple of years before Mouse realized the truth about herself.

On her second visit, Ellen mentioned that a friend of hers was hosting a small group of Lakota Sioux healers at her house and that she might find it interesting as one of their medicine men would be leading a small ceremony. She gave her the phone number of the folks who were facilitating the event and Mouse called as soon as she got home. If nothing else, she figured, this would be fascinating.

The event was not far from her home, so Bob dropped her off. The house where the event was held was a small, old farmhouse and by the time she got there, it was packed with people, most of whom seemed to know each other. She didn't know anyone, not even the hosts, but she knew their names and located them, introducing herself. The hostess told her to make herself at home, which was difficult as every chair in the house already had someone in it, as did the couch. The furniture had clearly seen better days and the house seemed unkempt. Mouse felt a little out of place and more than a little uncomfortable. The place was way too small to be holding as many people as it was holding, but the event itself was apparently taking place outside the house.

Mouse stood around, ambled a bit, and tried not to look as uncomfortable as she was and finally, the hostess returned with the good news that "the parade is ready to begin."

"The parade." That came as a surprise. The front door was opened, and everyone began to file out. Mouse, less than comfortable with being jostled simply because of her fragility, hung back a little and found herself at the tail end of the parade. At the head of the parade were ten or twelve young children walking in pairs. The girls wore flower wreaths on their heads, while the boys simply carried flowers.

The day was sunny, but there was heavy moisture in the air; there were no raindrops, but moisture quickly coated everyone. The glistening emerald grass was slippery as a result and Mouse took careful steps as the land was gently hilly. Soon the people in the procession were as wet as the grass. They were led around the property and someone up front was chanting in a melodious tone in a language Mouse assumed was Lakota. The march took them away from the house, then round toward the back of it.

As the children reached the backyard, they were led back into the house again while the rest of the participants kept up their slow, damp walk toward what was clearly a tipi. One by one, from her place toward the back of the line, Mouse watched as everyone in front of her bent down and sort of crawled into the tipi. That was going to be a challenge for her, but there was no turning back now.

When she got to the opening and her crippled-ness became evident to the folks who were holding open the flaps of the tipi, they did everything they could to help her in and slowly but surely, she got in and found herself amidst a sort of loose pile of people. It was dark inside, with only the light given off by a small bonfire outside providing a shadowy sense of the folks in the tent.

Once everyone was inside, a Native American man in traditional garb began what Mouse assumed was a prayer of some sort. His voice alone had a tone that was embracing and, somehow, wet and cold, in the midst of total strangers, she felt at home.

When the prayerful incantation ceased, the man spoke and asked the assembled group, if they were so inclined, to share what had motivated them to attend the ceremony today. A small voice—a woman's voice—spoke first. The facilitator handed her what looked like, in the dim light, a sort of a wand. She spoke softly, speaking briefly about some personal problems she was having at home. When she finished, the facilitator thanked her for sharing and noted that all of us wished her the peace she sought. Two or three more folks spoke up and shared before Mouse determined that if she were handed the stick, she would speak.

This was definitely nothing like Mouse had ever experienced before, but then... for the last year or so, there had been a lot of that in her life. She began tentatively, saying that she had been diagnosed with a fatal and incurable illness and that she had been fortunate enough to be accepted into a clinical study and that, in so many ways, her whole life felt up in the air. "That's all I want to say," she added. "Thank you for hearing me."

Her words were acknowledged, just as the previous speakers had been, with a simultaneous group "Ho!"

Not everyone in the tent spoke, but everyone who did was acknowledged with "Ho!" And when everyone had said their piece, the man who had been facilitating the process brought the proceedings to an end with a prayer in the language of the Lakota Sioux.

The rain had grown heavier while they'd been in the tipi and the earth at the entrance where they'd come in had turned muddy. One by one, beginning with the people closest to the opening, people left the tent. Mouse, who had struggled to crawl in and was now overwhelmed by the heat inside the tipi as well as the experience itself, slipped in the wet mud and had to be pulled out by some of the participants who'd already exited. They helped her to stand, and she made her way, shivering, to the back door of the house, following the trodden wet grass path that led there.

Someone had made a fire in the fireplace in the very small living room and the dry, toasty air permeated the whole first floor. Mouse made her way there and was pleased to find a large, cushioned armchair available. She'd been paper-towel dried off in the kitchen by a person whom she thought was probably the owner of the house, the woman who had led the 'parade' across the lawn. She sunk down into a well-padded chair, grateful for the comfort, and sat there staring into space as most of the people in the room were doing.

To her surprised amusement, a housefly landed on her right hand and began a sort of exploration of her crippled fingers. Mouse watched in a sort of fascinated trance. After the fly had competed for its digital exploration, it began its way up her arm, to the edge of her sleeve, then turned around and walked back down her arm. She was almost hypnotized by the fly's agenda-like behavior. When it reached the back of her hand again, it flew in front of her, landed on the back of her left hand and proceeded to walk up to the edge of that sleeve and back down again to her hand. She was, for no reason she could pinpoint, delighted. She was happier than she could remember being in a long time.

A bell rang, an announcement of food being dished out in the kitchen. Mouse wasn't particularly hungry and was wanting to sit with the delight she had, so she stayed put as the other folks milled around the small space, going into the kitchen to get something that looked like chili, then coming back to the living room to eat.

The children had been upstairs, and they came down to join the fray, many of them sort of nestling into their parents' legs as they sat on the floor beside them. The room was packed as tightly as a sardine can and the mood was growing joyful as the potent meditative effects of the sharing in the tipi transformed into casual conversations.

Mouse felt that it was probably time to give Bob a call and let him know that he could come to pick her up. She left her precious comfy spot and walked toward the hall in search of either the hostess of a phone, but as she rounded the corner toward the kitchen, she found herself in the small space between stairs that led up and the wall of the very short hall that led to the kitchen, face-to-face with an attractive woman of about her size who cocked her head and began speaking, "I heard what you said in the tent. Do you know anything about shamanism?"

Mouse didn't know anything about shamanism for sure. She'd heard the word before, but that was about it.

"Have you ever heard of a power animal?" the woman asked politely.

Mouse hadn't and her facial expression invited the woman to tell her.

In the native American traditions, the woman explained to her, they believe that everyone has a particular animal that resonates with their energy, that can be called on for assistance of what you might call a spiritual nature.

Mouse smiled. It seemed like a lovely idea.

"I help people to find their power animals," she said. "I trained with the shaman. Do you think that's something you might like to do... find your power animal?"

Who wouldn't? Mouse thought to herself and agreed promptly.

"My name is Deborah," said the woman. "Hold on a minute and I'll write down my phone number for you and we can set something up. I live near Philadelphia, well, in Philadelphia, actually."

"I used to live there," Mouse told her. "I won't have any trouble finding you."

Power Animals & an Invitation

Out of respect for the weekend, Mouse waited until Monday to call Deborah, who had wanted to set something up as soon as she could and before the week was out, there she was, at Deborah's house in an old residential area just on the edge of the city. It was a simple house, not too big and not too small, set on a narrow plot of land. Behind the house was a narrow, grass-covered yard and, at the far end of the yard, an interesting hut-shaped structure, "a kiva," Deborah had called it.

They would do the work she'd come for in the living room of the house, a room that seemed not to have seen much living, sparsely decorated, and sparely furnished in colors so neutral that they scarcely seemed color at all. Certainly, it was not distracting from the task at hand.

"They call this journeying," Deborah said. "You will lie down, eyes shut, and I will drum slowly, giving you instructions and information about how to proceed. It's a little like a combination of dreaming while you are awake and meditation, but with a guide."

Mouse lay down on the mat that Deborah had laid out for her and closed her eyes. Her arms rested loosely by her body. Deborah drummed a slow, steady beat. Mouse could feel her whole body relaxing, releasing the tension of having just driven to a place she'd never been before.

So relaxed that she was just about to drift off to sleep, she heard Deborah's voice softly inserting itself into what was left of her waking consciousness. "Remember," Deborah said quietly, "if at any point you are uncomfortable or want to come back, you can. Just let me know." Mouse nodded a silent assent.

"You are standing in a place that is well away from people and cars and civilization. It's a hilly area, not grassy, with dirt paths and trees around. Do you see it?"

Mouse nodded that she did.

"Walk little ways," Deborah added, going silent for thirty seconds or so. "Up ahead of you, there's an opening in the hillside. Can you see it?"

Mouse nodded assent.

"Is it on your right or your left?" she asked.

Rather than break her trance, Mouse wiggled her left hand.

"Good," whispered Deborah, more to herself than Mouse.

"If you feel comfortable," she added. "You can go in. This is a safe place."

Mouse walked in, looking all around as she did. She saw marks in earth-tone colors on the walls, but they were nothing she recognized. She continued her walk until she came to what seemed like a cave within the cave, a dark opening that she would have had to bend over some to get into, but it was so dark that she was disinclined to do so, the seeming reality of the waking dream overpowering what some people would call her rational mind.

Then she heard a noise, a soft scraping sort of noise that seemed to be emanating from the cave. Her breath halted and Deborah noticed immediately.

"What's going on?" she asked quietly.

"Something's inside," was all Mouse said.

"That's OK," Deborah reassured her. "Whatever it is, it will not harm you. However, it may appear to you. It is a symbol of your strength."

Mouse inhaled deeply. She waited, listening as the soft scraping noise grew more apparent and very shortly, there appeared an immense emerald green snake that looked to her to be six feet long or more. Slowly the snake moved toward her and rubbed against her leg, much as a friendly dog would. She had no fear. She felt that the snake's intent was, at the very least, a neutral one… more of sussing her out than anything else.

Then the snake raised itself up in front of her as if it were presenting itself, and its neck flared out as if the act were a symbol of its pride in itself.

She heard Deborah's voice, though it sounded as if it were coming from somewhere outside the cave she was in. She was asking Mouse if she were ready to return. Mouse nodded in response, not wanting to break the trance by speaking, and thanked her newly established powerful friend with a polite bow. Promising to see her again, she turned and left the cave, blinking her eyes into full waking awareness.

Deborah suggested that she rest a while and excused herself to make them each a cup of tea. Checking back a few minutes later, she found Mouse sitting up and invited her to the kitchen. They talked over tea and Deborah invited her to join a group that met monthly in the kiva in her backyard and who were, for the most part, healers. Mouse felt honored, although she had no idea why she would be included in such a gifted group.

Mouse went to the next meeting in the kiva, and the next, and the next. The attendees were, essentially, like-minded people with a strong attraction to shamanism and Native American ways. At one point, the same group of Lakota whom she'd met at first joined the group one weekend for an extended visit of sharing, song, and healing. Before they left, the women healers invited Mouse to come with them back to their home to train as one of them, but she turned down the invitation, fearful of being unworthy and fearful, as well, of what Bob's reaction would be to her leaving him for an extended time.

Not much later, she received a very different kind of invitation, more of a command, really. A friend's mother had been hospitalized in the local hospital, not far from Rick's house and she'd asked Mouse to accompany her on a visit. The woman's mother was unconscious and, as her friend pointed out, dying. "But she's just hanging on as if there were some chance for her and there isn't."

Mouse expressed her sorrow for her friend, who, to her surprise, said, "That's why you're here."

"I'm sorry," Mouse responded softly. "I don't understand."

"You can help her," said her friend.

Mouse stared at her; it was all she *could* do because she didn't know what to say... or do.

"You do this," responded her friend. "You'll know what to do."

Mouse had no idea why her friend thought that and so she simply stood there for a while, staring at the unconscious woman lying in bed. As she did, she recalled an unusual incident from a few years before when she'd first moved to the Cheltenham area.

She'd had a furiously infected tooth and was in a great deal of pain, but being new to the area, she hadn't any possible leads of who was a good dentist, so, knowing that her mother had been there for a while, she gave her a call to find out if she could recommend someone.

It turned out that her mother had a very good friend in the area who was, in fact, a dentist "...And a damn good one." She gave Mouse her name and number. Mouse was on the phone in a flash and, most likely because of the source of the referral, got an appointment for the next day.

When she arrived at the office—which was a home office—she was surprised to be greeted at the door by an elderly woman who was walking with—and hooked up to—a portable oxygen tank. The woman introduced herself and exchanged pleasantries with Mouse as they walked deeper into the house and ultimately reached a fully equipped dentist's office.

Mouse got herself situated in the chair and the woman performed the usual application of the bib before proceeding as would be expected. Mouse was acutely aware of the woman's labored breathing... but she felt something more. The woman was dying. Mouse felt it and she also had the sense that there was something holding her back, almost forcing her to stay alive. How or why she sensed this so strongly, she didn't know.

Because it felt correct to her, Mouse determined to have an unspoken conversation with the woman. Where that idea came from would always be a mystery, but it was there and as insistent as it could be. "So, I'm inside her head," Mouse acknowledged silently to herself once she'd made that connection. Then Mouse began a very one-sided and silent conversation with her, letting the woman know that it was okay to let go; that whatever the reason was that she was holding on so tightly to life, it simply wasn't necessary, and it certainly wasn't necessary that she should be in as much pain and discomfort as she was. "It's OK," Mouse silently, telepathically transmitted to her. "It's okay to let go."

The procedure was lengthy and when it was over, Mouse thanked the woman and bid her goodbye. Her mother called the next day, not to check up on her but to let her know that her friend had died in the night. Mouse didn't quite know what to think.

Now, here she was in a hospital, being asked to essentially do the same thing for this woman's mother. Well, she'd done it before... no harm trying, she guessed, and proceeded to do much the same thing with this woman's mother, whom she also didn't know at all, as she had with her mother's friend.

Her friend's mother died in the night.

Word got around and Mouse received another out-of-the-blue phone call, this time from a woman who knew a woman... and so on. This woman lived in a very upscale neighborhood in a grand house. She invited Mouse into the living room when she arrived and sat her down on the couch next to her, where she had a photograph album at the ready. She wanted, she said, to show Mouse something of her mother's life so that she could, in a sense, get a feel for what her life had been and from the looks of it, her life had been very comfortable and filled with family.

After this introduction to the woman she was about to meet, the daughter walked her back to her mother's room, where the elderly woman lay in an extravagantly beautiful bed, propped up on a number of pristine white pillows. The moment that Mouse stepped into the room, this frail-looking woman began attempting to sort of crawl up the headboard backward, supporting herself with her arms. She was clearly panicked and softly but loudly insisting something that was somewhat incomprehensible about making the light go away.

The only thing that Mouse could imagine was that she must have been emitting some kind of an aura that this older woman, possibly because of her closeness to death, could see and that it might have frightened her. Angel of Death or that sort of thing, perhaps. So, Mouse backed out of the room and, never having had to deal with anything like this before, just figured that what the older woman was seeing might have been her aura, and if that was the case, then perhaps she could sort of reel it in, so she set her mind to that and once she felt that she may have accomplished it, she took another shot at walking back into the room.

The older woman was fine. Whatever had happened was apparently no longer happening. Mouse took advantage of the calm, and as before, with her mother's friend, had a silent exchange with her. By the time she left the room, the older woman was resting comfortably in bed.

The daughter thanked her for her work and paid her. She called Mouse the next day to let her know that, in fact, her mother had passed in the night. She then invited Mouse to speak at her mother's funeral. Mouse was gobsmacked but felt as if she could hardly turn down the invitation and so, about a week later, she found herself in a pulpit in a church making a gentle speech based on all pictures that she had seen in the album.

It had gone much more easily than she had thought it would and the people who attended seemed genuinely grateful.

Word got around about her gift, and she found that she actually very much enjoyed the work. There was something about helping to set someone free that felt wonderful to be a part of. Although, there was one case where the family had called her in to work with their father, who was in a nursing home slowly dying.

When Mouse got there, what she discovered was a man who had no intention of dying. Yes, he was unconscious, but when she went to connect with him, there was a lot going on in there. The man was processing what she imagined had been his life and he 'told' her, at that level of consciousness, that he'd probably be about another two weeks and that his family should just get over themselves and "just relax." He was transmitting this information to her in a way that was almost funny and gave her a good feel for the family dynamics that were at play.

When she told them about it, she left out the "just relax" part.

Two weeks later, to the day, she received a phone call from the man's daughter to let her know that he had passed.

Strong Now

Despite the fact that her hands were still just as crippled as they'd been since the onset of scleroderma, Mouse was healthy. There was no trace of the disease in her body; her skin was testing as 'normal' on the once-dreaded pinch test, and her energy level was as good as it had ever been.

Bob lost his night job and found a day job, but the job with another printing company was in New Jersey. Since she was well, he said, she might be able to find a job there, too, if there was one that would allow her two days off a month for her photopheresis treatments. First, however, they had to find a place to live. An apartment or a townhouse was all they could afford, and that was fine. There were, after all, just the two of them most of the time.

They found a townhouse in Medford, not far from Bob's job and a whole lot closer to Augie and Gwen.

Mouse, who had no experience at all in the corporate world, had shown up for her first job interview in what she thought was a nice dress. The woman who interviewed her expressed her thoughts on Mouse's attire before she even addressed her skills, which were pretty minimal considering her limited—and rather unusual—work background. She was sure she'd blown it, but by the next week, she found herself working as a customer service representative for a company that manufactured medical devices used for post-op joint surgery patients. They had no issues allowing her two days off a month for her treatments. She was amazed.

Meanwhile, because her hands were still very crippled, she continued to be on the lookout for alternative approaches to restoring them to full functionality. As it was and would remain for the rest of her life, her fingertips almost rested on the palms of her hands, but she could type quickly enough using just the sides of her thumbnails that she had actually gotten a job that required no small amount of data entry.

Almost all the healers she had seen would tell her that she was a healer too, but she wouldn't have it. She didn't feel it and, as a rule, her feelings had served her well. Then, one day, as she was sitting at her desk, one of her superiors, one of the top sales reps for the company, came over to her desk and announced to her that she had a headache.

Mouse replied that she was sorry to hear that but that she did not have any aspirin, to which the woman replied. "You can fix this. I'll be at your house at 5:30."

Dumbstruck, Mouse just nodded. This seemed very creepy somehow, but she had no idea how to handle it. After finishing up the workday, she headed home and changed into more comfortable clothes figuring that this woman would just have to take what she got if, indeed, she even showed up. She'd have had to get her address from the records at work, but there she was at the door at 5:30, as promised.

Mouse let her in and, as she had no place set aside to do anything like heal someone's headache, she took her to the only place where anyone could sit with relative comfort, which was the makeshift living room they'd put together with a couple of mattresses and some throw pillows and she instructed her quest to find a way to sit comfortably so that she could get behind her, figuring that whatever this healing was going to involve, it would certainly involve her having to put her hands on this person's head.

Her guest positioned herself somewhat sideways on the mattress and Mouse knelt behind her, placing her hands on either side of the woman's head. She took a deep breath in and hoped for the best. To her surprise, she began to feel things—energetic things—in the woman's head. It triggered sensations she remembered feeling from the days when her small body was being assaulted in the woods. She recalled being able to feel what was happening in the men's bodies and instinctively knowing what to do to make them finish up what they were doing and get off her. *This,* she thought to herself, *was very much the same...* all she had to do was sort of follow the energy around, find out what it needed to do or feel to get out of there and kind of push it with her energy... and that's what she did.

And it worked. The woman thanked her, paid her—which was a nice surprise—and left.

All that Mouse could think was, *Well, that was odd.*

A few weeks later, she had another very different but equally compelling experience. She was returning home from work and noticed that the car in front of her had a very nice bumper sticker that she'd never seen anything like before. It was simple, rainbow colors in horizontal stripes. Hoping not to seem creepy, she followed the car into the townhouse development and, remaining in her car, rolled the window down so that she could call out to the young woman who had been driving as she got out of her car.

She asked her about the bumper sticker and the young woman told her that the rainbow was an emblem that was being used by the gay community to show solidarity. Mouse thought that was wonderful and a lengthy conversation ensued around the young woman's hopes and dreams for her life. She was an artist, she said. Mouse responded that she was as well. The conversation expanded. The young woman asked if she might come over sometime and see her work, to which Mouse responded that she could follow her home right then if she liked. And she did.

The townhouse was not large, so there was not a lot of work hanging, but the young woman seemed delighted. She stood for quite a while in front of a piece that Mouse had painted in the early days of dealing with scleroderma. The title of the piece, Seven Reasons to Live, was part of the work.

"What is this painting about?" the young woman wanted to know, so Mouse told her the story of her illness and her desperation and wanting to end her life. Tears appeared in the girl's eyes and ran down her cheeks.

"I have been thinking about suicide," she said softly and went on to explain her struggle with her parents over her sexuality. It had been weighing very heavily on her as she really had no place else to go, but Mouse's story had so moved her that she said that she felt stronger.

They talked more and before she left, Mouse offered her the small painting. The young woman was beyond delighted and left in a distinctly improved state of mind.

Then, a few weeks later, something even more unusual happened.

Mouse was still doing yoga every morning. While she hadn't been able to do it physically when her whole body had been so constricted by scleroderma, she'd made sure to go over it in her head on a regular basis. She didn't want to lose it. These days she was doing it, as she always had, first thing in the morning, even before breakfast.

One weekend morning, she was mid-practice, in plank pose, when an immense burst of light and energy sort of exploded directly in front of her, literally throwing her backward.

Then there was a voice, "I am an Embodiment of the Light."

Mouse had landed leaning back against the box spring and mattress on the floor that was serving as a bed. The huge light was behind her now, seeming to support her. The next thing she knew, her chest was being opened up as though it were a trunk, and out of her flowed a slimy stream of black creatures about the size of raccoons but more like amorphous platypuses in shape. They spilled out of her chest, onto the carpeted floor, then up the wall to the large window that was there and somehow slimed their way through the narrow opening and out.

Suddenly, there was a very loud voice that seemed to be coming from everywhere, "Now you have to do for others what has been done for you."

And it was over.

Mouse was stunned and trembling. She lay there for a long time, conscious only of her own breathing.

Once she was restored to what felt to her as if it might be normal, Mouse began to wonder what, exactly, was meant by "Now you have to do for others what has been done for you."

All she knew for sure was that an enormous amount of what appeared to be really vile energies had been released from her body, and all she could think was that she'd just experienced a sort of exorcism. Was she supposed to be doing exorcisms for people? It seemed like a pretty big step up from all the "You're a healer" messages that she'd been getting… that said, considering the delivery, this message was pretty hard to brush aside.

Ultimately, she determined that research of some sort was in order. The first thing that she did, because she had a sneaking suspicion—an old memory fragment from Catholic school—that Saint Michael had something to do with exorcism—was to go online and read up on him. Indeed, she discovered, exorcism was one of his more well-known gifts. For whatever reason, this relaxed her a little bit. She felt validated in her knowledge which felt to her that might be an indication that she was heading in the right direction.

The next thing she did was to investigate the process—or processes—involved in dispossessing someone of malevolent energies. There were many lanes to go down and many different approaches. She found one that resonated with the "gifts" that she seemed to have access to, like being able to sense and feel energies in people, and she purchased the materials that were being offered. She studied like she'd never studied before. She'd hated studying in school; it seemed so useless; either she knew the information, or she didn't. No amount of "cramming" had ever served her. This, though, drew her in and kept her reading.

Ultimately, once she felt as if she'd taken in all that she could, she began to wonder, if this was, indeed, a skill, how would she go about making her skill known? She thought about the local spiritual/metaphysical magazine that came out monthly and on her next trip out, she picked one up. It looked like the perfect venue, so she created a small, affordable ad and submitted it.

Free At Last?

On the day before her next scheduled appointment for photopheresis, Mouse received a phone call at work from one of her sisters. Her father, her sister told her, had died.

Mouse, momentarily unhinged by the unexpected news, let out a wail so loud that people came running from everywhere... from the offices and the warehouse and the loading dock. When she finally looked up from her desk and turned slightly, she became aware of what she had done, although where it had come from and why it had come, she could not say.

She swiveled her chair around to face them and said, very softly, "I'm sorry... my father died." Murmurs of sympathy came from everyone, but where, Mouse still wondered, had that sound come from... and why? She loved her father and he loved her... he'd had a stroke some time ago, so his death was no surprise, especially with the history of drugs and alcohol he'd managed to maintain.

Someone had contacted her immediate superior, who came to her and told her to go home, but Mouse didn't want to go home. She'd been made manager of her department by then and felt that she'd simply like some time to compose herself if that was alright; that she'd rather get back to work as she knew that she'd be away for the next two days for her monthly photopheresis treatments.

She had calmed herself by then and her manager knew her to be dependable, so it was agreed, as it was already early afternoon, that she could see the day through.

Everything went normally for the rest of the day. She barely cried at all. And in the morning, she set off, in rush hour traffic, for her monthly visit to the hospital, which, by now, she very much enjoyed. It was like a mini-vacation every month punctuated two really big ouches.

Mouse was in for a surprise this time, though. The pinch test went as usual; except for her hands, all the skin on her skin was now "normal," but when she arrived at the check-in desk, after checking in, Bill escorted her not to one of the rooms of that hallway as was usual, but took her on a walk to a part of the hospital where she'd never been before; in fact, she hadn't even known it existed.

The room they entered looked like a small hotel room, not a fancy hotel room, but a far cry from a hospital room. There were framed landscape paintings on the wall and two beds, one that was clearly awaiting her and the other a perfectly normal twin bed with a tapestry-like bedspread on it. There was no window to the outside, though, as there was in the clinical unit, so the room had the feeling of being at a complete stop.

Mouse was confused but said nothing. Bill was not forthcoming. He pulled the curtain around the hospital bed so that she could change into the standard hospital gown, which she did. Once she had slipped into the bed, she gave him a call and he pulled back the curtain, moving UVAR into position beside the bed.

He said nothing. She watched.

He got her hooked up to UVAR and she watched as her blood began its circuitous journey through the winding tubes.

Then, the doctor who had first interviewed her came into the room as he usually did, just to check in and see how things were progressing. After the usual exchange, he began to explain that because pretty much no one except for her had experienced any substantial changes in their condition that the clinical trial was being defunded.

He apologized, looking as if his heart was breaking. Mouse felt sorry for him, seeing the sorrow in his eyes, feeling the sadness he felt. He had told her, long before, in their first interview that the people who had quit the treatment had all died shortly thereafter. She knew that he thought that now she would die as well and that it was all he could do not to cry... but she knew that she was fine, and she told him that.

"I'll be fine," she said. "You don't worry about me."

He looked even more sad then, so she stopped talking.

"Is there anyone you'd like to be with you for this last treatment?" he asked softly.

"Yes," she said without a moment's hesitation. "My daughter." Gwen was a hop, skip, and a jump away in school at the University itself. He took her name and told her that they would find her.

She thanked him as he left and all he could do was nod. She felt terribly sorry for him because she knew, without a shadow of a doubt that she was— and had been for a long time—fine. But she also knew that her daughter, if she knew what was going on, would want to be there and it would be a joy to spend at least some of the day with her.

The treatment went as easily as it always did, the only difference being that she wouldn't be there for another treatment the next day. There were tears on parting, but Mouse was quietly thrilled. On the way home, she decided to stop at her favorite gem and rock shop to pick up something special that she could wear to celebrate her healing and closure, as well, for this part of her life.

At the shop, she chose a small sterling silver bird claw pendant that she could wear as a necklace. The claw—which reminded her of her hands—was clutching a many-faceted quartz crystal. It was perfect; she left the shop wearing it.

When she pulled in at the front of the townhouse, she was surprised to see a minivan parked where she would normally have parked. She pulled in next to it and as she got out of the door, she saw one of her sisters exiting the van. Looking more closely, she saw her sister's two sons strapped into their car seats. Her sister, who had been alerted by Gwen, had come to give her a hug, after which they chatted for a bit.

The talk turned to her boys and Mouse commented that one of them reminded her of their maternal grandfather and uttered something under her breath about what kind of a person he had been, joking that she hoped that he hadn't returned. Her sister, in reply, and not knowing anything about the horrible abuse Mouse had suffered at the hands of their grandfather, made a comment about their own father being an abuser and when Mouse looked befuddled, commented, "Didn't he get you?"

The next thing that Mouse would recall was that she was holding herself up by clutching the edge of the kitchen table as she watched, in her mind's eye, a kind of filmstrip reel showing her, in detail, moments from her childhood with her father 'teaching' her how to give him pleasure, and then images in the woods, strapped down, with Annie, and a kind of rack off to the side with small living things—she couldn't tell what for sure—perhaps they were infants?—strapped to it. Fires were all around. It was just like the awful dreams she'd had in college... it was the same subject matter, only far more vivid.

She stumbled across the small hallway to the tiny living room area and fell on one of the couch mattresses, her mind reeling, replaying the living nightmares over and over.

Just as quickly as one chapter in her life had closed, another was opening.

That evening she called her mother. "Yes," her mother admitted, she knew about the incest. Then Mouse related to her the part of the 'newsreel' that she had not reported to her siblings, the part that had so disrupted her dreams when she was younger, the part about the rituals in the woods of which she and Annie had been unwilling witness to.

To her surprise, her mother wailed loudly. The sound was much like the cry she herself had released at work only days before. Then, she cried loudly, "Not my father; don't tell me those things about my father!" and slammed down the phone.

About two weeks later, in the late afternoon, Mouse received a phone call at home. When she picked up the receiver, she heard a woman's voice asking for her. Mouse acknowledged that this was she, whereupon the woman identified herself as her mother's secretary.

This couldn't be good, thought Mouse to herself. In her life, she'd never heard from any of her parent's secretaries.

"Your mother just called me," the woman began, "from the airport in Santa Fe to ask me what she was doing there. I'm concerned." She went on to say that once she had told Polly why she was where she was, Polly had asked where she should go, and her secretary had given her the name of the hotel where she'd be staying. She'd told her to write it down.

That was the first indication of the end of a brilliant mind. Polly deteriorated and would soon take up residence with one of her daughters.

Expanding

It was decided, after numerous back-and-forth phone calls and emails, that all of the siblings might benefit from some kind of group processing under the wing of a wise counselor. Those of the family with such contacts, which, by this point, included Mouse, reached out and a suitable person was found who felt up to the task.

The counselor interviewed each family member privately, then hosted a group meeting where almost everyone was given a chance to speak openly with everyone else. Annie, by now, was living in California, far from all the family drama, which was just as well as many of her siblings were far less than comfortable with her.

It was a bonding experience that lasted longer for some than for others but proved valuable in different ways for each person that had attended, although

Mouse still felt distanced. She had been her father's favorite and it had been difficult to ignore that.

Since her father's death, Mouse's subconscious mind had gifted her with some dreams that she'd rather not have had, dreams that echoed her infancy with her grandparents and, later, around the strange ceremonies in the woods. She sought help, first, from a hypnotist, hoping that "going back" might provide her with more clarity, clarity that might help her address the underlying anxiety she carried about her childhood experiences in the woods.

The hypnosis didn't go so well as, when the counselor tried to walk her back in time and she got to the woods, she panicked, in a trance, and began furiously to try to escape what she imagined was happening and even attempted to climb a wall, trying desperately to get away.

She didn't go back. One person that she saw had suggested that she blow up photographs of her parents and grandparents' faces, glue them onto a large box and then bash them in with a bat, yelling or screaming or saying whatever she needed to say. She tried it out in the back of the townhouse one afternoon, but she was unable to summon up any emotion at all. She gave up and determined to focus, instead, on pursuing the path that St. Michael had laid out for her, to just get on with her life. That was all done, she'd thought, over behind her. She was okay, not great, perhaps, but good enough.

Eventually, her ad was published and she sought to obtain some kind of realistic certification that would allow her to perform as the healer that so many people and one really large Embodiment of the Light had told her that she was. She applied to a four-year program to obtain a Ministerial Ordination and an honorary Doctor of Divinity degree and sought out someone to initiate her into the hands-on healing energy called Reiki. Then, at least, she wouldn't feel like a poser.

The ad brought her more business than she had expected, so she was able to pay for her schooling without interfering with the domestic budget. She developed a client base surprisingly quickly and eventually, after still more training, was able to add Feng Shui to her list of offerings. Finally, she felt more comfortable with herself in this role than she'd ever imagined she could.

One day, seated on the living room mattress, a woman who came to her for regular "tune-ups" came walking in through the open front door and, without even saying hello, tossed a pamphlet into her lap, nodding her head in a way that indicated, "Read that now."

Mouse read the headline on the now unfolded sheet of beige paper: "Walk-Ins for Evolution." She glanced up at her client, who simply nodded back at her as if to say, "Keep reading." Obediently, Mouse continued reading. The essence of the piece was that there exist, on earth, a certain number of people who have come here to assist humanity, each in their own particular ways. These people are soul/spirit beings, as we all are, but these particular people are soul/spirit beings that have entered the body at some time after the birth of the body, freeing the original soul/spirit inhabitant to continue on its particular path.

This might happen because the original inhabitant had satisfied all of its karmic obligations and had no need to continue in human form. Or it might happen because of a previous agreement between two beings. Or it might happen because the projected life events ahead might be something required by the incoming soul/spirit but not required by the current resident. At any rate, it is an agreement between souls, not a take-over, and the goal is always to add value to humanity in some way, no matter how small.

She finished reading. Her life suddenly made some sense.

She looked up at her client, a woman who would one day become one of her closest friends, and said, "I am one."

"I know," answered her visitor. "But I knew that you didn't... that's why I brought it for you."

The childhood birthday party on the lawn suddenly made sense.

"And I know when it happened!" she gleefully responded, signaling her friend to sit with her so she could relate the story to her.

Two Steps Forward and Oops

Mouse was pretty pleased with the way that her life was going. She was helping people; she was doing good things; she had ceased being wildly flirtatious and was dressing appropriately to her status as an ordained minister and healer.

Then, unintentionally, her old ways reared their ugly heads. One of her clients had recommended her to a friend, a man who had endured some serious mental issues with depression and had, at one time, been hospitalized as a result. He also had a critically disabled son who was frequently hospitalized and a wife who was not emotionally equipped to handle all that.

Her client had suggested to him that he might benefit from seeing her. Ted was one of those rare men who seemed to be almost as sensitive as she was. He was kind and gentle, intelligent, and understanding. He was also seriously overweight. He'd suffered abuse as a child and had mentally and physically collapsed under the weight of it and he was still carrying it.

Working with him brought Mouse in touch with her own, still fresh, emotional wounds and he was so very much the emotional opposite of her husband, who'd also been abused as a young boy, that she bonded with him quickly. That bonding led to a brief physical relationship, but one that lay heavy on her as the moral inconsistency sat heavily on her mind. The relationship did not last long; it couldn't, but it served its purpose, waking her up to the inconsistencies in her marriage that had led her to find comfort elsewhere.

Moving

As Mouse's practice grew, Bob determined that it was probably time to move into larger quarters, though Mouse could not see why. They had enough room.

But he was insistent and set about finding something they could afford in the same area as he was still working nights at the printing company. It took a while, but he finally located a house that he felt would work well. It had a large first-floor room in the back that she could use as her workroom. It had a bank of windows that opened on a scruffy grass-covered backyard, but it served to fill the room with light. There was a small dining room and kitchen and a good-sized living room that he set up as their offices. The master bedroom and an extra bedroom where the kids could stay when they came to visit were on the second floor.

The first floor, though, was clearly a place of business, not a home, and not a place for entertaining company. One lovely thing for Mouse was that, unlike their previous residence, there were sidewalks that led all around the neighborhood and she could safely take walks on a regular basis.

It was in that house that Mouse experienced one of the most vivid visions of her life. It happened on the night of September 10, 2001. Unable to fall asleep, she had decided to move herself to the kids' room across the hall so as not to disturb Bob. Still unable to drift off, she decided to try a treatment on herself that she would normally be using for clients. It was a combination of color and fragrance that came in small glass bottles. It was a beautiful system in which the clients themselves would choose the bottles that attracted them, explore with her what the chosen bottle 'meant,' and then, if they desired, they could purchase the bottle and take it home with them to use in whatever way they had determined that it should be used, on the skin, or in a bath, or just for meditation.

She knew instinctively that night that she needed the bottle called The Christ. She went down to her workroom, shook the bottle as was required, and then applied it on her temples, over her heart, and on her wrists. She then headed back to the kids' room, where she lay herself down on her back, much as she might if she were on a massage table.

Then, almost immediately, she saw, as if she were a bird in the air, the entire United States as if it were made up of billions and billions of tiny twinkling lights.

What is this? she wondered to herself.

And then there were larger flashes... three of them. And then it was over. But it kept replaying in her mind's eye until sleep finally found her.

The next morning, she was on the phone with a client when the woman on the other end of the connection simply began shouting, "Get to the television... go there now," and hung up. The panic in her voice was practically palpable, so Mouse ran upstairs as she knew that Bob would be watching the morning news in bed as he always did.

The screen was filled with the face of some innocuous-looking white man whom she did not recognize. His voice was filled with a combination of fear and confusion.

"Who is that man?" asked Mouse.

"That's your president," answered Bob.

"What's going on?" she wanted to know.

Bob started to explain but stopped short. "Listen," he said.

She did and panicked, and then she turned to Bob. "There's going to be two more," she said.

"What do you mean?" he asked. "What are you talking about?"

"Two more," she repeated... still stunned. "Two more things... this isn't the end."

He stared at her blankly as she left the room to find herself someplace quiet to sit and process what had happened and what she knew about what was going to happen.

The day before, she and Bob had gone to the beach at Sandy Hook in New Jersey. Walking back to the car from the beach, lugging their fully-loaded beach cart along the narrow boardwalk through the low-lying dunes, Mouse's eye had been caught by two very large somethings that seemed—to her—to be gleaming, off to the right in what she knew to be New York City. She stopped.

"What's that," she asked him, pointing towards the city. "Those black glowing things, I've never seen them before."

"That's the Twin Towers," he'd responded with the kind of tone that people often use when they're addressing a child that's annoying them. "They've always been there. They're not black."

Mouse sat alone for a long time, trying to understand why she had seen what she'd seen, wishing she had known what it had meant.

A Brief and Unpleasant Winterlude

A few winters before, Bob, who had by now become totally enthralled with the idea of nudism, something Mouse could only blame her own curiosity for, as it had been she who suggested, on a quick trip that they had taken to New England, to visit with her sister, that they check out a place that she had heard of called Martha's Vineyard. It was a nude beach. She had read about it somewhere, years before, and was curious. That was her nature.

There are probably very few men alive who would not have taken her up on following her curiosity straight to the nude beach and Bob did. It turned out to be a very small place and somewhat challenging to access as it involved descending a muddy and somewhat rugged hill to get there. It was there that Bob fell in love with the idea of being naked in nature; Mouse, not so much.

Mouse was not a great lover of sand in general; it irritated her, but he'd been sold on it, so much so that every summertime thereafter, they made regular Saturday and/or Sunday trips to Sandy Hook, New Jersey, which was the only naked beach within driving range.

On their first winter in their new house, Bob determined that he would like to celebrate the new year by visiting one of the many nudist resorts that he'd read about in the nudist magazines. The resort was in Florida. One of the women that he worked with at the printers also ran a part-time limousine service. The plan was that she would drive Mouse and Bob to the airport and then home again when they returned.

Mouse was not as fired up about this as Bob was, but she knew she was going, so there was little point putting up a fuss. The trip was fine. The resort was what anyone might expect of a place, calling itself a resort in the middle of a city. It consisted of a motel-like setup that had been erected around a couple of large swimming pools and hot tubs. Mouse tried to look on the bright side: at least there was no sand.

The place had a very clublike feel to it. It seemed as if most of the people there knew each other and most of the women were fairly obviously ignoring Mouse. She'd attempt to open a conversation and be blatantly ignored. Bob, on the other hand, was involved with volleyball, and racquetball, and badminton, was having a great time. In addition, the maids, all women of obvious Latin descent, as Mouse was.... and looked, especially after spending all of her summers on the beach, also tended to blow her off when she'd ask for something. She was even more uncomfortable there than she'd been in dancing class decades before.

She could hardly wait to get home... but the trip was a nightmare, a plane ride into a snowstorm and then being driven home in the worst of it. It seemed as if the extra money she was bringing in was being used to entertain her husband, but then, she was very happy doing what she was doing, glad to be useful to others, and enjoying her sort of local celebrity, so she felt as if she had nothing to complain about.

More Moving

She was never entirely clear about what happened when, one day, not long after their trip to Florida, Bob told her that they would have to find someplace less expensive to live. She'd been making even more money than she had been the year before and her client base had expanded, but he seemed almost panicked about the situation. Tending to the money was his business, but her income and his were both steady and reliable.

It would be years—decades—before she discovered that he had been secretly playing the stock market with her income and that, in addition, he had never paid into social security for her. She had asked him outright about it one day not long after the last move and he had lied to her, telling her that he had been.

But at that time, she knew nothing about the household finances. That wasn't her job. She held a yard sale to try to limit what they would have to move into as they were going from a two-story house to a two-bedroom condo. The condo was in the same area, close to his job at the printing company, so she'd be able to maintain her client base... or so she thought. But shortly after the move, Bob suggested that it would be a good idea for her to go to work at the printing company as well.

But why? she wondered. And then, he let her know that they were moving to the night shift, so she could see clients in the daytime. She could only see one or two clients and still get some rest, and so that's what she did. Mouse was nothing if not compliant. She'd learned early how to accept the unacceptable.

She had become friends with a couple of her clients and their occasional company meant the world to her. Bob, meanwhile, had taken up volleyball in his spare time, so she saw rather less of him. In what little spare time she had, she returned to painting and drawing, which, for the most part, she kept to herself, but one evening when Bob was out with his volleyball friends, feeling as if she really needed to do something out of the ordinary, she poured paint all over her belly and then pressed herself up against a canvas. She loved what happened and embellished the imprint. The end result tickled her... was her... that belly that had once been taut and now, two pregnancies and many years later was soft and wrinkled, was like a living history.

When the work dried, she wired it and hung it across from the small room where she saw her clients. She thought that it would make a strong statement for other women to see.

She had a dream that night in which a voice gave her instructions on how to help clear the body of old and outdated information that it was carrying, old emotional cellular programming, in other words. The voice told her that she needed to teach her clients how to do it because they couldn't always afford to visit her. That way, too, they could use the technique in their lives to help their children release the kinds of childhood trauma—small and large—that can linger in the cellular consciousness and sometimes go on to disrupt their adult lives.

The voice then described in detail how and why this technique worked. It made sense. The voice then told her to get up and write it down, which she did. She then emailed her clients with the instructions so that they would have the technique all written down should they want to use it. It was a mild concern that she would lose business, but she didn't.

Bob, who was by then playing volleyball three nights a week, hadn't seemed to take much notice of the painting because it hung in the narrow hallway that led from the bedroom to the living room area, which had been converted into an office, so the painting was not in his direct line of vision. Also, he had become preoccupied with the young wife of one of the volleyball players and was regularly emailing her, to her husband's vocal dismay.

Mouse knew about this because he'd told her about his predicament. He didn't understand, he said, why the husband was so worked up. Mouse told him that it didn't really matter that he didn't understand that he was being asked to desist, that he should simply stop because he'd been asked to. Mouse was furious, but she managed not to let that color her tone. She was more concerned, at this point, for the young woman and her relationship because Bob seemed to have lost his mind a little bit.

Later that week, while he was away at a game, Mouse determined that she had better do something she never would have dreamed of doing before and check out what was on his computer. She was expecting to find the exchanged emails, which she did. They amounted to the young woman virtually begging him to stop emailing her and his pathetic, overly dramatic return emails explaining his position of, essentially, being enthralled with her.

As Mouse scrolled down the list, though, she stumbled across something unexpected, an email from what sounded as if it were a movie-making enterprise of some sort. Already farther than she felt comfortable being, she figured, *Why not?* And opened it. What she saw appalled her. The email contained a few links with titles like "Mandy and Susan Get it on."

Further down, an invoice from the same enterprise. So, this was what her 'extra income' was going for?

Porn, thought Mouse, *obviously.* That came as no big surprise, but she thought that she'd click on the link and see exactly what kind of porn he was watching. It turned out to be "teenage girl-on-girl action." She wasn't thrilled, but she was even less thrilled when she saw what this was costing. No wonder they'd had to move!

She confronted him. He responded that watching porn was no big deal and she shot back that spending their money on it when, apparently, things were so tight, though, was kind of a big deal. The discussion went nowhere.

Then, one day while she was out, Mouse's beloved belly painting caught his eye, and she returned home to find her work splashed with a huge swath of red paint that covered easily a third of the painting. It was acrylic paint; there'd be no way to remove it. The piece was ruined.

That's what did it.

That's when her tolerance crossed the finish line.

She researched the local area to find the D-I-Y divorce center that she knew she'd seen somewhere, found it, and purchased the kit, which came complete with instructions on how to file and where to go to do it. The form was simple and straightforward; she filled it out and filed it the next day.

Then she began making plans.

The first thing she did was to let her daughter, who was living in Rhode Island, know what she had done and that, with her help, she'd like to move there to be nearer to her. She knew that was asking a lot of a single young woman with a demanding job, but her daughter was enthusiastic, which felt, to Mouse, like the most love she'd had directed her way in a long time.

She then contacted one of her sisters, whom she knew had a truck and a husband that would be willing to help his wife help out her sister. She needed to move, she told Inez and asked her if she and her husband could help her out. She didn't have much, but it was more than would fit in her Buick sedan. Inez was fond of Bob, possibly fonder of him than of her sister since Mouse had been her father's favorite which, despite his death, still annoyed a number of her siblings. But she agreed and within a week, Mouse was on her way to New England to put down new roots and start all over again.

She had dreaded telling her boss at the printing company as she knew very well that he had gone out of his way not only to employ her but to put up with her husband's shifting work requirements as well. But he was not only understanding, he also offered her the opportunity to work remotely for the customer service department. He had been excited to have remote workers and had tried establishing an office in India at one point, but the time differences had caused numerous issues. She was thrilled.

The move took place on the Friday before Memorial Day weekend. Mouse had everything of hers—which wasn't much—packed and ready to go. The mood was somber, and the day was hot. The trip, thankfully, went easily. Another one of her sisters, who lived nearby in Massachusetts, met them at the old house where Mouse's new apartment was a three-story climb up. That was the most challenging part of the trip. The old wooden stairway was narrow and a person toting a large box could barely fit in and then, of course, the large box made the stairs difficult to even see as the lighting was fairly dim.

The apartment itself, though, was like heaven, especially compared to the condo she'd just left, where the only view was a parking lot. There was one small porch just off the kitchen where she could hang out her laundry to dry and another larger porch just off a living room that was all windows in the treetops where she took to having her breakfast in good weather. There were two small bedrooms, one of which she could use to see clients if she could get any or paint if she couldn't, and a very small bathroom with a makeshift shower in the tub that was just fine with her.

The kitchen was the first room one entered, and it was the largest, with an immense amount of storage space, more than she'd ever need, and a stove that served double duty as the heater. It was old and odd and awkward for sure, but, come winter, it did its job just fine.

As luck would have it, Mouse did not get to stay in Rhode Island. The economic crash of 2008 had caused the printing company that she worked for to have to downsize and they needed her to come back. Because there were literally no jobs available in the Providence area, she had no choice but to return. This time, however, there was no one that she knew that could help her move, nor could she afford to hire a mover, but her boss took the initiative and told her that he and a good friend of his would rent a truck and come up and drive her back. Now the only issue was, where would she stay?

Bob had kept in occasional touch with her via email, so she took a chance and wrote to him asking if he could please find her a place to stay. Once he had found a place, she let her boss know, and the arrangements for moving were finalized. She was heartbroken. Her life, while simple, had been immensely gratifying there. She had found a woman's group that met on Friday nights to dance; she had acquired two or three clients; she saw her daughter numerous times a week; and had even attracted a male admirer whom she had no interest in whatsoever, but it had been nice to be noticed.

A date was set, and her boss and one of his friends—coincidentally, a former client of hers—arrived late one afternoon in light snow. The truck was loaded so that they would be able to get a start first thing in the morning and, hopefully, avoid the worst of the snow. After loading the truck, her boss and his friend decided to walk out into the local area and find themselves a bar, which they did. When It was that they returned, she had no idea, but they were ready to go bright and early in the morning.

Overnight, there had been a blizzard. The snow was a good six inches deep, but her car had already been prepared for snow and the truck had come that way, so they set off for a drive that would ordinarily have taken about six hours but ended up taking ten and left her with a seriously cracked windshield—from a ricocheting shard of ice—that would have to be repaired. Luckily, the damage was on the passenger's side.

Her boss had made arrangements for Mouse to stay at the home of one of the other employees of the company for that night, a woman that she knew well. They left the fully loaded truck there, all ready to deliver her and her belongings on the following day to the new apartment in which she would be staying.

Exhausted, Mouse slept soundly, despite the fact that she was sleeping in a windowless cinder block basement on a mattress on the floor. She felt a little as if she had been jailed, but she was not awake long enough to care.

First thing in the morning, her boss and his friend arrived to drive with her to her new lodging, which was in a small town—more like a small city, really—not too far from the printing company. It was an old industrial town, not pretty, but she could afford it on her printing company paycheck, which was all she'd have until she could re-establish her healing practice.

She was the first one up the stairs and was somewhat dismayed to find chicken bones littering the stairs on the way up. It rang a kind of danger bell in her mind. *Drugs, maybe?* Something wasn't right here. She knew it... but there was nothing she could do about it at this point.

She continued her walk up, bones in hand so that she could dispose of them. She opened up the door to a strangely laid-out little apartment. The door opened to a narrow hallway that led to the left and to the right. To the right was a small room with one small window. To the left was an entrance to a small bathroom, the entrance to an equally small kitchen area with a tiny window oddly placed about an inch from the ceiling, and, at the end of the hall, another small room that was presumably to be used as a bedroom.

The bedroom had two small windows, neither of which offered a particularly inspiring view, but that was okay, thought Mouse, *I'll just curtain them.*

Once the men had moved everything in for her and she had thanked them profusely, which was all she could offer them, she sat down on the mattress that would serve as her bed and gazed, as if in a trance, down the small hallway to nowhere. She was not happy; she was not sad; she was a little bit angry at Bob, but because there was nothing to be done about that, she let it go, got up, and began to unpack.

With each move she had made, there had been a little less and a little less to move, so it didn't take long to put things in order. Exhausted, she fell asleep on the unmade mattress.

The next day was Sunday, giving her a chance to put things in order. If there was one thing that Mouse's conscious mind craved, it was order. She had grown up hearing her mother's mother say, more times than she could count, "There's a place for everything and everything is in its place." Whatever that gene was, she'd gotten it.

It was a strange place, no doubt about it. In the tiny kitchen, which consisted of, basically, a refrigerator, a four-burner stove, and a kitchen sink, there were two small overhead cabinets and the tiniest window that Mouse had ever seen, which sat well above her head. It was the strangest placement for a window that she had ever seen. It was also the smallest window that she had ever seen in a for-real house. From it, she could see only the sky.

By day's end, everything was in its place. Mouse slept soundly, waking just in time to make it to work on time and, in many ways, grateful to be back in territory that she knew well. At least she wouldn't have to navigate her way around; she knew where she was.

She slipped back into place at work, keenly aware of the resentment of the two women who were the other members of the customer service department. Her leaving had caused them to have to work more than they were used to or cared to. Generally, they enjoyed lively conversations and shopping online. Except for circumstances where "the head of the department" was called for to handle some unpleasant situation or another, Mouse was usually the one handling the day-to-day business of testy or persnickety customers. She stepped back into her normal role, grateful for the work because she liked to work and she liked to help people.

By days end, though, she was glad to head back to her ratty little apartment. She had to make arrangements for telephone service and find out where she could get her windshield replaced. She had things to do. However, when she arrived at the corner where the narrow brick building that she'd just moved into the day before was, the area was roped off with the bright yellow caution tape that the police use to keep people away from something not-so-good. Police cars and fire engines lined the sidewalks.

What on earth? was all her mind could manage.

She held down the tape and stepped over, knowing that would alert one of the numerous... police? Firemen? She couldn't tell. All sorts of different vehicles were randomly parked up and down the street. But someone, she knew, would object to her crossing over the flimsy barricade, and someone did. Before he had an opportunity to speak, she addressed him. "I live there," she said, trying not to sound too agitated. "What's going on?"

"Eh!" exclaimed the man with a slightly disgusted air. He was dressed in what looked like some extravagant kind of all-weather gear and boots. "Some little druggie on the third floor was shootin' up, sitting on her sink, and the pipes gave way. Place is drowned."

"Ummmmm..." was all that Mouse could tentatively manage.

"Y'won't be gettin' in there until tomorrow at the earliest. Gotta check the safety of the structure an' all."

There was nothing she could say... nothing she could do... but she'd have to find someplace to spend the night at the very least. Everything she owned was in there. The woman with the cinderblock cellar lived farther away than she'd have liked to travel, besides, the woman had a strange vibe. Mouse wasn't sure what it was all about, but it made her uncomfortable. Then she remembered that the woman who'd, long ago, it seemed, driven her and Bob home from the airport in a snowstorm lived in the next town over, even closer to work.

She pulled out her cell phone, called work, and asked one of the nightshift typesetters to see if they could find her phone number, which they did. Her name was Debra and she treated Mouse's request as if she'd just been offered a pot of gold. She had a bedroom in her basement, she said, and Mouse was more than welcome to stay there. The directions to her place were so simple that Mouse didn't even have to write them down. In less than ten minutes, she was at Debra's house, where Debra stood outside, in her driveway, welcoming her in.

After Mouse had satisfied Debra's curiosity about what on earth had happened, Debra told her that the small town was well known for drug activity. She was mildly appalled that Bob had thought that it would be a good place for Mouse to live. She'd ordered Chinese food from a local take-out place and told Mouse to settle in while she ran out to pick it up.

Mouse broke down and cried tears of gratitude as she wandered inside and plopped down onto Debra's couch, sighing heavily, hoping things would get better.

They did.

Their hours were slightly different, so they drove separately to work, but they had dinner together every night, watching every episode of NCIS that had ever been made. Both enjoyed cooking and took turns at dinner. Life was peaceful once more.

Mouse had a bath and bedroom in the fully furnished basement. The floor was wall-to-wall carpeted, so she could do her morning yoga comfortably. She was hesitant to paint but got to work on a vision board. She had created two of them when she was in Rhode Island and as she set about scanning through magazines for appropriately goal-oriented pictures, it occurred to her that, if Debra did not mind, she could perhaps pick up with some of the clients she'd had before she had fled. There was room to do that in the big rec-room sort of area in the cellar that she had to traverse to reach her private bed and bath.

Debra didn't mind at all, so Mouse got started by offering a class on making vision boards. Of course, the women who responded wanted to know if she was still practicing hands-on healing. One thing led to another, and her practice soon returned. She felt fulfilled and content and reveled in the sister-like relationship that had developed between Debra and herself. She had no plans to be anywhere else or live any other way as long as Debra would have her.

Spring came around, and while taking in the greening of the grass and flowers budding, Mouse suddenly felt, as if out of nowhere, that as soon as she could afford it, she deserved a vacation. Life had been pretty challenging for the last little while and she wanted to have some fun.

Back in the days when she and Bob had been spending summer Saturdays at the nude beach, Bob had learned about a clothing-optional resort in the hills of West Virginia. It was called Avalon. They had an area for camping—which was not his speed at all, but they also had what they called "The Lodge," which was, essentially, a motel-like building with a huge great room at one end that served as a restaurant and entertainment venue. It was there, in the great room, that they held dances with a professional DJ every Saturday night… and that's exactly what she felt that she needed: cutting loose, naked, on a dance floor.

Bob had been no dancer, but he had enjoyed watching, specifically, naked women dancing, but Mouse discovered that dancing naked was about the most freeing experience she had ever had! Of course, being the possessive person that Bob was, he'd refused to allow her to get on the dance floor alone, knowing that she'd, no doubt, catch someone's eye and be asked to dance. Happily, though, one Saturday night, they happened to share a table with another couple and the husband of that twosome also did not dance. It was a fortuitous match.

Mouse, knowing full well that a single woman at a clothing-optional dance would be more cheese than Mouse, called her old friends and told them of her plan to spend Memorial Day weekend at Avalon, entreating her friend and fellow naked dancer, Laira, to entice her husband to join her at the dance that Saturday night. Laira was delighted. They hadn't been there very much recently, and she looked forward to the opportunity.

Mouse and Bob had been to Avalon so many times that she almost didn't need a map to get there, though she had one, just in case.

She had arrived on Saturday afternoon of Memorial Day weekend; the dance wouldn't be until the evening, so after settling herself and resting up a bit from the ride, she decided to take a little walk around the premises to see if anything had changed in her absence. The grass was lush and green, perhaps a little unkempt, but then, the whole nature of the place was one of relaxation.

She walked out the back entrance of the lodge in order to take a nice longish walk over to where the building that was referred to as "the barn" was. She stepped up onto the slatted boardwalk that led to the side door of the barn and as she did, she noticed a single piece of a puzzle lying in the grass.

That's odd, she thought to herself as she stepped off the path to pick it up. She carried it with her on the rest of the walk. Once upon a time, a few years before, when she'd been there with Bob, she'd also found a piece of a puzzle, that one she'd found beneath the window of the lodge room that they had been staying in and she had picked it up and taken it home to add to her box of odds and ends that she used in creating art.

After a short walk and as much sun as she wanted to absorb, Mouse returned to her room for a little nap before dinner. Alone at dinner and knowing no one, she ate in silence and returned to her room. She was feeling a little disappointed at the lack of camaraderie, but then, as she knew, most of the people there knew most of the people there and she hadn't been there in quite some time. But she was there to dance and that was all that mattered.

She fell asleep on her bed for quite a while and when she woke up, the dance was already underway. She found her friends, Laira and Frank, seated at a table near the bar, and after a little pleasant, if loud, conversation, Laira and Mouse hit the dance floor as planned. They talked through the slow dances and danced through the fast ones while Frank nursed a drink at the table.

As Mouse was watching some of the dancers on the floor enjoying a slow dance, a man approached her and asked her to dance. He was very polite and pleasant looking, so she thanked him for the invitation, turning him down while letting him know that she had come there very specifically to dance by herself. He nodded and smiled and returned to his two elderly friends who were standing not far from the table, near the bar.

A fast song came on next and so did the polite and pleasant-looking gentleman.

"I thought that may be because this was a fast dance…" he stopped purposely before finishing his sentence, knowing that she would know that he understood—or thought that he understood—that she might not have wanted the kind of close contact that the slow dance would have required because when you're naked, that close contact is closer than usual.

Mouse smiled at him, tickled by his persistence and delighted by his understanding of that particular subtlety... and she turned him down again.

"I really did come here to dance by myself," she repeated, smiling. He was kind of adorable.

"Okay," he responded in a surrendering tone. "But if you should feel like a cup of coffee in the morning, I live in the house at the top of the street that bears your name."

He gave her a slight nod, returned to his friends, bid them goodnight, and left.

Laira and Mouse danced themselves out and Mouse thanked them enthusiastically for making the trip and helping her out, after which they left for home, and she returned to her room for a very good night's sleep.

In the morning, after she'd done her yoga in the room and had her breakfast in the great room, she took notice of what a gorgeous day it was. The sky was clear, and the temperature was warming up quickly. She had to return home that day, she knew, but she thought, *perhaps I'll take a walk... and maybe get a cup of coffee.*

Donning her socks and a pair of sneakers, she set out in the direction of the street that bore her name. She knew where that was because Bob had driven both of them up there a few years before to see this special house that she was now going to visit on her own.

That trip to the house—the one with Bob years ago—had been an interesting moment for her. As they had driven up the hill that led to the house, which was situated on the top of the hill, a thought had popped into Mouse's brain. *I deserve to live in a house like that,* she had thought. That thought was immediately followed by a second one. *If you did, you'd be living in it.* Chastised by her own conscience, and knowing that her conscience was correct, she let the thought go.

Today though, she was going to at least have coffee there.

She arose, did her daily yoga practice, then popped into the great room for some breakfast. She stepped outside to check the weather. It was already hot, and it was only about 9 o'clock, but she'd very much been looking forward to a nice walk as she had to take a long car ride home that would take a few hours, so after breakfast, she went back to her room, donned a pair of socks, put on her sneakers, and headed off. The walk, she knew, was only about a mile, but she'd neglected to bring along her water bottle, forgetting, in her excitement for this small adventure, how parched a walk in the hot sun can be, forgetting also that the walk was, for the most part, going to be uphill.

She walked along the dirt road that connected the resort with the clothing-optional community where Rob lived, passing by a large pond where she observed a very large turtle lounging half in and half out of the water at the pond's edge. Some hawks flew overhead. *This place,* she thought, *was a nice blend of the wild and the civilized and she fancied herself somewhere in between.*

By the time she'd reached the street that bore her name, she was in dire need of water. It felt as if her tongue was going to stick to her palate, and the street that bore her name was on a good-sized hill... going up.

By the time she reached the house, she was desperate for water. Never mind coffee. She walked to the door and knocked.

Nothing.

There was a car in the driveway, so she was pretty sure that he must be there. She knocked with more vigor, but still, no one came to the door.

Her temper began to rise a little and she then pounded on the door with all her might.

Nothing.

Mouse wasn't having it. She was going to get a drink of water if she had to break a window. She began a slow walk around the house, looking in every window she could find, seeing no one. Finally, about halfway 'round, she heard a very regular, very mechanical sound that she recognized, from Bob's gym activities, as an exercise machine. The sound was coming from above.

She moved into action, searching among the many trees that surrounded the house for a fallen branch that would be large enough to use to bang on a second-floor window. The branch had to be long enough to reach the window but also narrow enough for her crippled hands to hold. It didn't take long to find the perfect instrument, though, as the house was set on the edge of a densely wooded area.

She walked over to the area from whence the racket seemed to be coming. The noise was relentless and loud; she'd have to make an impression, so she wanted to get as much of the branch visible in the window as she possibly could. Mouse was neither tall nor heavy, so the task was a challenge... but she did it. One! Two! Three strikes and that was all she could manage, but the next thing she knew, there was his face at the window, a look of utter confusion on his face... until her face registered. He signaled for her to go around the house, back to the front door, and by the time she got there, he was there to open it for her, just on the verge of laughter.

"Water," she said. "I need water."

He stepped back from the doorway to allow her entry and guided her to a small spiral stairway. The area she was walking through, she noticed, was not 'finished' though the stairway was. As she ascended the stairs, her eyes met an almost-finished round room filled with the morning light. It was a purely wonderful space; she'd never been in a house like this. She expressed her delight, and he went on to explain to her how the house had come to be and was, in fact, still becoming.

There they sat, exchanging information, Mouse, naked save for her socks and sneakers, and Rob, who was also wearing socks and sneakers but was, as well, fully attired in sweats. Oddly, she was not the least bit uncomfortable.

The house, she thought to herself, was a lot like her, an ongoing project. No wonder he'd been drawn to her… He liked a project! And no wonder he'd known how to engage her interest, he'd remembered her from years before.

She drank her water while he made coffee. He was preparing for a trip to Italy with his daughter the following week, he told her and expressed an interest in seeing her when he returned. He'd enjoy going up to New Jersey, he said, as he'd heard about Sandy Hook but, though he'd grown up just outside of New York City, had never been there.

Mouse had to get going. She had arranged to visit one of her sisters on the way home and very much did not like driving in the dark, so Rob drove her back to the lodge in his golf cart, which was the standard means of transportation within the resort. They parted ways, having exchanged contact information and Mouse drove back to Debra's, stopping at her sister's on the way.

She was a little excited but determined not to get carried away.

She was delighted to get a postcard from Italy and further delighted to get his call when he returned to the states. They set a date for a trip to the beach for the following week. She would discover, on that trip, how devoted the man was to his Avalon community as he'd brought with him flyers for an upcoming event that was happening there and took time out from sunbathing to walk around distributing them among the countless sunbathers... until he was stopped by a patrolling policeman.

Apparently, it was illegal to "advertise" anything commercially on the beach as it was considered National Park land. Mouse had been going there for years and had never known that. Rob got off with a reprimand and the rest of the day was spent with Mouse mostly relaxing and Rob alternating between the ocean and the beach. He was, she learned, an avid scuba diver. By now, she knew that he was a swimmer, a scuba diver, a person who liked to ride horses and someone who loved to travel. The list gave her pause. She enjoyed none of those things and had no interest in learning to enjoy them. But him... oh, she liked him a whole lot. Not just the physicality of him—he'd been a wrestler in his youth and had the very kind of body she'd always been attracted to—but his demeanor, his politeness, his many very obvious skills. Sigh... *what was he seeing in her,* she wondered.

When they got back to Debra's, they showered—separately—and dressed and were about to settle down on the couch in the 'entertainment' room outside her basement bedroom where Debra's kids and grandkids used to gather to party before she'd moved in. She stood at the bar, pouring them sodas. When she felt him come up close behind her, his hand on her shoulder exerted a gentle pressure that implied that he'd like her to turn around.

She was facing him then; he wasn't too much taller than she was.

"I'm going to kiss you," he said in the most gentle but somehow intentional voice she'd ever heard. She felt a feeling flow through her body that was like nothing she'd ever felt, and she tilted her head back ever so slightly to receive a soft and slightly lingering kiss that brought their bodies together as though they had melted into one.

They slept together that night... just slept... and Mouse experienced a feeling of safety that she had never before known.

She liked it... a lot.

And that was the beginning of a love story, the sweetest story of Mouse's life.

Epilogue: Healing

"There are more things on heaven and earth, Horatio, than are dreamt of in your philosophy."

-Shakespeare, Hamlet

About four years into her marriage to Robert, Mouse began to exhibit some very unpleasant intestinal issues. Always preferring alternative approaches, she sought out a local acupuncturist. During the years just after she'd endured the worst of scleroderma, she'd had experiences with four different acupuncturists, each of whom had felt that they could assist her in regaining some flexibility in her fingers. None did, and two of the four had seemed more like sadists than healers. But the other two were genuinely, obviously concerned with finding her at least some level of comfort. So, when she found herself in need of what she felt must be some sort of re-balancing, she asked around and received, from two sources, very good recommendations to a woman named Dixie.

Dixie treated Mouse and Mouse was thrilled by the lack of pain involved. She was also thrilled to find that her intestines, which had been a factor in her desiring treatment, had been restored to normal functioning. But a very strange thing happened that night when she was asleep... or, rather, when she awakened from sleep in the middle of the night to find herself thrashing wildly underneath her husband, who was repeating, over and over again, "It's alright... it's alright..." And then, "It's okay... you're safe."

Her dreaming mind had her running through the woods, holding tight to her sister's hand. Maybe they could get away... but Annie was resisting, as Annie always did when anyone tried to make her do anything, but Mouse, kept going, determined to rescue herself and her sister... until she was awakened by Robert's attempts to calm her.

"It's okay… you're safe," he said more softly as she calmed down and her mind entered the reality of husband… bed… safety.

Dixie had asked her when they'd finished the treatment that day if she might like to return to do some work on her still crippled hands. Mouse had told her that she would have to think about it, as her previous experiences had put her off more than a little. But the dream that had followed her initial treatment so impressed her that there were no questions in her mind to answer. This woman had skills that ranged far beyond the ordinary.

What transpired, instead, was about four years of working with Dixie, whose skills managed, bit by bit, to allow Mouse's aging body to finally release the deepest, darkest memories and emotions that her body had still, unconsciously, been holding onto. And, while her fingers never did release their claw-like shapes, a vigorous blood flow had been restored and her fingers no longer turned blue at the least drop in temperature.

By the age of seventy-five, Mouse was finally as free as a person could be and she would tell you that only that freedom could allow her the confidence—and fortitude—to share her story with you.

About the Author

Victoria Pendragon is the author of Sleep Magic, Surrender to Success, and Being in a Body. Those books are the result of having lived the life that is detailed in this book, Scorpio x 10. The "incurable" autoimmune disease—progressive systemic sclerosis—a disease that turned her body, inside and out, into scar tissue and, by all rights, should have killed her, allowed her to live, learn about the healing process, and ultimately reach a point where she felt confident enough to share a story that speaks to some of the unavoidable consequences of Childhood Sexual Abuse.

www.ingramcontent.com/pod-product-compliance
Lightning Source LLC
Chambersburg PA
CBHW072043110526
44590CB00018B/3016